A Journeyed Lifetime within 33 Years

by Jennifer Parks

The contents of this work, including, but not limited to, the accuracy of events, people, and places depicted; opinions expressed; permission to use previously published materials included; and any advice given or actions advocated are solely the responsibility of the author, who assumes all liability for said work and indemnifies the publisher against any claims stemming from publication of the work.

Dorrance Publishing Co
585 Alpha Drive
Pittsburgh, PA 15238
Visit our website at *www.dorrancebookstore.com*

ISBN: 978-1-6853-7005-3
eISBN: 978-1-6853-7862-2

Dedication

Oana Brodnicki, Andrea Griego & Nicole Aderhold – for being the creators of an idea for a book, and encouraging me to recognize that I have a lot to offer for others, even if it is only stupidity

Kim Galvan – my twin incarnate, who has provided me with the recognition that I am fully deserving of my personal opinions. Without you I would not be confident enough to write a book, nor would I have embraced my truly unique method of conversation and thought.

Contents

Introduction

Some idiot friend of mine decided to flatter my ego one day with some crazy notion that I needed to write my life story down on paper. The following day another person did the same. I brought the notion back to my husband (who can be way too supportive for his own good), and of course, he agreed with the idea. Then a third friend suggested the same. Within a few weeks, I felt honored to be admired as someone who had experienced a series of events that were worthwhile enough to write a book. But by no means does this, or my sorted tale, make me any more or less important than the next. Some readers might vehemently disagree with my perspectives, my judgements, and my overall outlook on life. I hold no grudges. In fact, quite the opposite.

We are all on a journey that takes us from one place to the next, but a sequence of events is fully dependent upon the time and place of every occurrence. Meaning, in an imaginary world where everyone is the same physically and mentally, if one were to adjust the timing of a significant life event, the impact and perceptional changes would vary significantly from person to person. You could have twins live through some shocking revelation three days apart from each other, and while they are wired the "same", their outlook on life would vary considerably. Maybe it is having one twin watch the other go through something they themselves had happen a few days later. Or vice versa. There is no way to know why we are all different and affected differently from outside stimuli, but one thing is for sure: we are all here just the same as the next. Not one person is more valuable or less valuable. We are all humans, experiencing the life cycle at different rates of speed, and in varying levels of intensity. With that in mind, make no mistake: I am the average person sitting next to you.

It can also be said that it isn't just what you experience in life that makes you worthy, but how you develop yourself to maintain a positive outlook (or in my case, a severely fucked up outlook), despite the multitude of rides life can take you on, both with and against your will. I am no master at handling life's curveballs, but I truly hope any reader can take away something from this sorted mess of my lifetime!

The intent behind this book is to utilize comical expression to inspire others and publicize awareness about common feelings and struggles that happen to many. My belief is that there are far too many things that are common, yet they are kept within and guarded, and very rarely ever talked about on a public forum. As a social entity, we fail to humanize independent occurrences that can wear a person down physically and emotionally, and as a result we have bred this intolerance to life's most challenging moments. We have evolved from generations where talking about emotions and admitting truths about oneself is not appropriate on a public level. Through the development of their descendants and evolution we have experienced a cultural shift from enjoyment of life to concentrating solely on monotony success and tragedy. We have also bred this efficiency-based world for ourselves that has worn people thin. As a result, the human psyche is over exhausted, both physically and psychologically.

It is not reasonable to believe any human can endure running at 110%, 24/7. We are simply not wired that way, nor are most things in nature. We are, after all, beings. We fall apart. We break down. And it is only through maintaining our physical and emotional health that we can continue to stand back up. This explains why a younger child is capable of healing better and faster than someone older. Why hangovers are reserved for anyone past 30 years of age. Why wisdom is lost on the elderly, and why youth is wasted on the young. We are part of the creation of a natural cycle. A life cycle. Nevertheless, the emotions that exist within us are just as important as the stimulation that drives us. We must learn to take care of ourselves, both internal and external.

Readers will find that through a variety of experiences, I have come to ascertain realizations about life, myself, and community (both family and friends) that I rely on for prolonged health and wellness. Some might call this an autobiography of sorts, but I chose to stray from the traditional theme for a book of that nature. There will be both positive and negative encounters described in some detail, and comical tales of woe. Prepare yourself for an interesting journey through the perspective of this individual's thirty-something year old existence. Enjoy!

Chapter 1

The Demise of Humanity: A Tale about Fallon & Kit10

Very seldom do pet owners experience a lack of pure unadulterated entertainment and devotion from their furbots. This has become a consistent experience throughout my life, and from a very young age I intended to learn as much as I could about the mental capacity of both cats and dogs. Unfortunately, I have spent my time researching a vast number of topics, other than this. The interest still maintains itself, as does the curiosity, but I firmly believe the downfall of the human race will be at the hands of all things furry. While one may not initially understand my mindset, I hope that by the end of this chapter it will soon make sense!

All pet owners have tripped over their respective animals. Be it a large or small cat or dog, we have experienced this. Although there are a number of possibilities that could result from this action, there is one of mine that stands out in particular. I was innocently walking down the hallway towards the bathroom, when my cat ran out of my bedroom and ran in front of my path. She hit my foot as I lifted it to take another step, and I soon found myself faced with a severe dilemma. Do I try to catch myself as I fall, alter my path downward, or do I come to terms with the result as it stands, potentially injuring both myself and the wall ornaments strewn about my hallway? Within the few moments it took for my raised foot to touch the floor, I had already decided to commit to saving myself. However, in this action, my rather large and overweight 15-year-old Golden Retriever made an attempt to chase after the cat. The dog had walked down the hallway ahead of me, and as I rounded the corner to the bathroom, and tripped over the cat in the same movement, my dog turned around. It was at this moment I realized that I was doomed. There was no coming back from this reality. Because as sure as I had experienced a number of times before, my dog was extraordinarily capable of taking me out.

In the past we had been playing together outside, however this time there were additional facts to consider. The tile floor, for example, the edges of the wall corners and picture frames, the fact that there were two door frames side by side, just wide enough for my head to get stuck between, and the list goes on. What I had not anticipated is that through the dog making contact with my other foot, as I made another step, I would lose my balance so drastically that I would stammer forward, while moving side to side, through the bathroom door and towards the toilet. I felt like a drunk person trying to regain balance, aside from the fact that I had not had a sip of alcohol. As I took the next few steps, I decided that my fate was sealed, and as my head entered the rim of the toilet bowl, I made one last ditch effort to grab onto the edge of the toilet, in an effort to prevent assassination by germs, and potential drowning. As my entire body weight was thrown forward and downward, I managed to muster all the potential strength and save myself at the last minute. Success!

Success can be measured in a number of ways. Success is something that varies based upon an individual's goals and based upon an individual's sense of humor. It can be the little things that makes or breaks a human, just as it is the larger things that can inspire and motivate additional efforts. I was elated at this success. So much so that I almost cried, and to anyone who knows me it takes a considerable amount to get me to tears (unless I'm intoxicated, in which case...I'm fucked. Proper fucked, as it were).

One of the most valuable lessons we can have in life is knowing that when you are legitimately doomed for failure, there may always be a light at the end of the tunnel. Anyone who has experienced depression or suicidal ideation can understand this. Anyone who has lost a child and/or miscarried can relate. But in that moment, I was victorious. I did not let the furbots take me down. I remained strong,resilient even. I remained their master. And there is something to be said for the amount of pride I maintained by not being engulfed in toilet water, face first. The excitement of being able to relay this encounter to friends, with a validated sense of accomplishment is probably one of the only reasons I have admitted this experience publicly.

Any other day, Fallon and Kit10 would raise hell together. They seemed to have a love hate dynamic that would rival them all. There were days when the young cat could not stand the old dog's energy, and she would frequently flee the area to avoid being wacked in the face with the dog's tail. Yet there was an undying amount of love between these two furbots. Whenever it was outside time for the three of us, Fallon would watch the cat like a hawk. Her ears would raise, a huge grin plastered on her face, and she would literally pounce like a deer through the grass to make sure the cat got back inside and didn't wander. Of course, Kit10 could not stand this process, as it would occur numerous times no matter how long we remained outside. I would swing on my "back porch swing", the dog would walk the perimeter and the cat would find alternative places to hide or climb to avoid being chased, like my husband's axe throwing station outside and yes...you read that right! He bought throwing axes and needed a place to practice, so he took a wood pallet, and propped it up with a random wood stump he found along the ground somewhere and made himself a target. Kit10 would climb that in the hopes of being queen of the world! And also, to avoid a dog who was way too energetic for her taste!

Other times, the cat would show rare signs of true affection. I have caught her grooming Fallon's face, cuddling inside her nook, and on one occasion I made the mistake of separating them during a ten- or twelve-day trip. I came home a day and a half before arranging Fallon's return home, and Kit10 was deeply distressed. At first, I thought it was just because she had been alone and missed me. But I soon came to realize that her constant meowing was not due to me being evil, it was because I had taken away the other furbot friend of hers. Sure enough, the second Fallon walked into the house in her happy-go-lucky way, the cat shut up. And what a way it made me feel to know that I was somehow inadequate! That my return home had rendered her utterly confused at the mystery of the disappearing dog. But I appreciated the fact that they had that bond. I appreciated the fact that despite Kit10 being incredibly docile (never hissing or with claws out), she was able to understand the relationship she wanted from the dog, even if that meant tolerating Fallon's antics.

Speaking of such antics, every morning Fallon would lose her ever-loving mind over the fact that I woke up. As her master, it is normal to assume she would have some level of attachment to me, but like clockwork, the second I would wake, she would get overly excited. Sprint down the hallway to her dog bed, flop on it, and proceed to shake all over. I've never seen a dog do this, and considering Fallon had hind leg soreness, it was a miracle to me how she managed. The next step was to go outside for a potty break, which she greatly appreciated, and following our return inside, the same activities with her dog bed would commence. I would eventually fill her dog bowl with food, Fallon would wait patiently in front of it for loves and kisses, and then to make sure Kit10 got her food treat and was happily drinking water next to the dog bowl, before starting to eat her own meal. And God forbid if I wasn't present every time to witness the entire series of events! Following her meal, Fallon would walk back towards the bedroom, and sprint down the hallway to her bed again, proceed to flop over, kick, wiggle, and snort all in one moment. This could last anywhere from a few seconds to minutes. Sometimes, she would get encouraged to continue longer than just a few minutes, and wear herself out. I'm ordinarily not opposed to dog's getting their energy out, but on a few occasions, Fallon would render herself incapable of breathing. Yes, this dog just got herself so wound up that she is now wheezing and hacking up a left lung.

Another time the loving Fallon would lose all mental capacity was on the sight of visitors, or should I say smell? If the doorbell rang, I was done for. If someone knocked, I was screwed. If anyone was to come to my house, I had to make sure Fallon was outside prior to them arriving, otherwise, the dog would attack with love as soon as the door was open. She would shake and jump and turn belly up, and if someone stopped touching her, she would repeat the cycle until someone paid attention. Being that Fallon was a whopping 70 plus pounds, this can get exhausting for any visitor to put up with. Especially if she got herself to the point of hacking up again. I discussed this issue with the vet, who seemed unmoved by my concerns. So, she told me there was a dog trainer that could help with the issue. Instead, I opted to do it myself, and slowly but surely, Fallon learned that after a few minutes it was time to willingly go to her bed. Despite her obvious facial guilt trips to be let off her bed, she stayed on her bed while the grownups talked for as long as she could take it. Which usually didn't last but a few minutes, before she was back off of it and run from visitor to visitor.

But the end all be all moment between these two, is when I open the door to my bedroom, and I see them both tag teaming me with a look of accountability a parent gives a kid who just got peanut butter all over the home. Somehow, I failed them because they were outside the door, when my husband shut it. By some stretch of the imagination I was now to withstand the pain that I sowed by failing to come out of said door sooner. To make matters worse, if I intended to get up shortly before walking through the door, I was a goner. After I would feed and potty the dog, if I dared return to my room and put clothes on to leave the house (which is strictly anything but comfy clothes) I was met with a severely disapproving brood. The dog would tuck tail and walk into the closet where she would peer out from under my dresses and skirts and give me the guilt tripping look of the century. Or she would stand like she was preparing to enter the closet and stare blankly at the wall. The cat would find a way to be under my face every chance I got close to a countertop. Occasionally she even let out sounds of displeasure either before I left, or when I got home. As if to say, "Bitch! Don't leave me home with crazy again!". After a few minutes of loves, both pets would calm down for the most part. The dog would still trail me to the door and give me one last sad look as I reached back to grab the front door and shut it behind me.

One day, I decided to put shea butter on my legs, following a relaxing shower. As I began with the right leg, both my cat and dog walked over and began licking my leg, before successful application. So, I raised my leg, not thinking much of it, and finished applying the lotion. As I put my leg back down, both pets commenced with their individual licking routines. The cat took one side, and the dog took the other. I managed to fight my way into applying my shea butter to my left leg, after a few weak pushes and assorted movements on both legs. By the time I accomplished the left leg, the right leg was now licked clean of all lotion, requiring another layer. As the pets moved quickly on to my left leg, I realized I was doomed, if I was to stay in this seat and work on this sorted project in front of both pets. So, I did what any normal human being would do in the situation, I got up and ran into our office and closed the door so they could not follow me. My husband, who was sitting at his computer looked at me like I had a unicorn horn growing out of the top of my head, and asked, "What are you doing?" I simply replied by telling him the pets would not allow me to apply my shea butter without licking it off. He started laughing and continued his game.

On another occasion I tried to apply the same lotion on my legs when the dog wasn't around, thinking I could handle my cat, right? Wrong. She quickly woke up from a dead sleep, went over and began her cleaning ritual. I just sat there after completing both legs (she licks a lot slower), and just let it be. I figured once she was done, I would reapply and that would be that. Once she completed with me, she soon commenced to licking herself, from head to literal toe, because apparently my body was so dirty after a shower and lotion application that it made her filthy. So, I reached over, grabbed the shea butter and reapplied. I have never in my life seen a docile cat so disdained. Who knew this could be the end all be all for cats? She quickly stopped licking and returned to my legs, at which point I started to realize just how tiresome this was for her. She began to give me looks, and heavy sighs, and slow long licks as if to inform me through nonverbal communication exactly how taxing my reapplication was to her. I started laughing. In my head I was contemplating normal cats and their fascination with cat nip. My cat hates cat nip. In fact, I smeared it on her once, and she got sick. Not that the cat nip did her in or anything, but she literally got sick. Two medications were required multiple times through the day, for ten days. And even with a docile and unaggressive cat, there is nothing more complex than trying to hold a cat that doesn't like being held, force medication syringes down its throat and feed it medicine in the hopes that the majority will actually get consumed. She would do this weird gurgle thing that rendered most of the medication all over her face, but I figured during grooming, she'd digest it. After the second dose on the first day, I realized how doomed I was.

This cat was giving me hateful faces that made my insides turn. Especially since this same animal would then hide from me for hours on end, and then sleep on me at night. I contemplated the real possibility that she was considering how many ways she would plot my demise when I least expected it. And the same can be said for my attempts at reapplying lotion. It was very evident to me that I was NOT to do this again. For a moment, I thought it was actually humorous to know that this could be the one thing that would act as my cat's kryptonite. Some people put cucumbers behind their cats while they are eating. Others border abuse and feed their cats alcohol, and meanwhile all I did was apply lotion. Who knew!?!

Chapter 2

Misunderstood Glory

It is not uncommon for small town Americans to avoid visiting other cities, states, or even countries. I was afforded the opportunity to explore parts of the world seldom travelled. During my childhood my parents initiated a relationship with USAID and Research Triangle Institute, that landed us in Indonesia. My father worked, while my mother spent time working on her PhD dissertation. I spent a considerable amount of time learning the language, the culture, and things that any ordinary kid would learn. Throughout the four years we lived there, we would take trips to experience various forms of architecture and urban and rural designs, since that was my father's profession and purpose for us living there.

As a young child myself there were things I was never able to understand about American culture, because I lived in Indonesia during a pivotal time in life where one begins to understand social interactions and cultural influences. Along with not having a clue about American geography, there were a number of things I missed out on, with regards to the traditional U.S. preteen experience. I also was exposed to things that mystified me, especially since others my age were unaware of the capacity for variation in the world. Namely, the difference in religion and religious requirements, the role of women in society, the capacity one will go to in order to save a child that is not their own, and the dedication of a small community in strengthening each other. All of these things were new to me and helped me gain insight well beyond my years. The mature perspective that developed as a result of my travels created an internal struggle. My largest complaint about my younger years was that people would not take me seriously, when realizing my age. This was something I carried through to my older years, even as a twenty- something. Once I reached the ripe old age of 30, people started to listen and show respect.

But to get back on topic, these experiences I was being subjected to, for example the small-town communities within a larger country, bewildered me. In the U.S., we all assume a relative similarity. People might have a common religious theme, be it Christianity, for the majority of the country, but things like accents and daily tasks may fluctuate. In Indonesia, there was so much more variation between one town's beliefs and principles. For example, Tana Toraja is a place I continuously talk about. The way houses were shaped was most unique, and their spiritual beliefs about souls remaining in the top tiers of the house with the living is extraordinary. Their houses are built on stilts because of the likelihood of flooding, and the graves for their loved ones' remains were built into the side of the nearby mountains. Some were so old that you could see skulls in the entrance holes that had worn away over time. In addition, they were running out of space for their dead to be buried. If memory serves, they started to double-up on graves, in order to accommodate the generations to come that would eventually pass away. Although much of the land, homes, and area has been infiltrated by outsiders and revamped by funds, there was a unique and complete sense of pride in their separatism from the rest of the country. Their purity in rituals and lifestyle remained so. While I have not gone back, I know through photos and press releases that this purity is threatened, to the utmost degree, as are much of the smaller, more rural locations in third world countries.

One of these such locations is Bali. Although it is well known for the resorts, the beaches, and as a vacation destination. There was a time that it maintained its purity. Driving down small dirt roads and back--alley passages that inspire the question of whether or not two vehicles are truly expected to pass each other within the designated width. a And then, realizing that if unable to fit, one car is surely to fall off the cliff that exists almost before the road stops, and nature begins. And strolling along such avenues are people, of both genders, dressed in sarongs and traditional attire (as w westernization is yet a concept), with baskets on their heads. The kids find mud holes to play in, while mothers walk to and from the local markets. Vendors try and steal your every rupiah (the currency), and require you to walk away before giving in to your price. Or the smell of the environment that never affects others that have lived there all their life, but as a foreigner it stands out as a foul odor. Sure,, disease could spread through the community, but after a lifelong submersion in that environment, who can truly remain alive without building an immunity or tolerance to the most common parasites or germs that inevitably stretch from one end of an island to another. They have each other to live for, and their lives to enjoy. And while working hard is a prided and valued concept, there is little to no pressure on expediency, or accomplishing the unimaginable. They are satisfied with their existence, if not fueled by it.

It pains me to see the changes, just by witnessing stories and photos. Bali is not the only location that has been scarred by the damage of w western clothing, religious standards, and it is only the beginning of the downfall of various historic cultures. Because trust me, whatever we may value in our history, there are a multitude of cultures and faiths that were present long before the U.S. was established. And religion! (Need I mention the obvious?) Being a Muslim in this world, especially in the w western r regions, was never popular. In fact, I would go so far as to say it was frowned upon. I In today's international community there is a vast misconception regarding the true beliefs of the Muslim faith : what it entails and all that it requests of their followers. That is all perceived as hateful, yet they are one of the most docile and peaceful lifestyles. Indonesia itself has Buddhism and Hinduism as the other two most popular religions (aside from Christianity), both of which value personal reflection, peace, acceptance, and forgiveness. Not to mention the affiliation between terrorism and the Muslim faith. When dealing with a religion that's reach is as vast a as that of Muslim influence, you will find extremists. You will find misunderstanding. You will find hateful opposition. Yet it is only the scholars who fare to give time to research and discovery. Which results in a larger population completely oblivious to reality and truth.

Throughout my undergraduate studies I was interested in psychology and sociology, and it was no surprise to me to learn about the in-group/out-group philosophies proffered by wise men. It is the ideal that anyone foreign to your norm must therefore be a threat. And over the course of time, I have witnessed groups and individuals alike worn down by the fears they envision without provocation. And for some non-instigating opponents, they are unfortunately eliminated, and unable to withstand the external pressure from others.

Yet Indonesia maintains some of it cultural attributes, and hopefully will continue to do so. They possess pride in presenting Gamalan performances to visitors and amongst themselves. They take pride in having foreigners welcomed into their respective houses, and even the more scholarly citizens as visitors. As a result, there are festivities that will rival any traditional American gathering. The object is to put on a performance so magnificent that it cannot be topped. This is exuded by performances of music, dance, and puppetry. Food is shared, and historic stories are narrated during the depiction of dance and puppetry. And accompanied by music played by only the most renowned Gamalan orchestra members, sought from all islands within the span of Indonesia's territory. Anyone who goes into this experience with their eyes wide open, knows that it is truly a blessing and honor to witness this rarity. As western cultures infiltrate, the likelihood of finding such festivities increases. Be it from learned professionals passing away before passing the torch, so to speak, or because of cost and effort, to put on a show. Although their social hierarchy and respect for others perceived as elevated in status still remains, there is a dwindling sense of pride in continuing older traditions.

Another cultural custom for foreigners is to hire on workers of the host country decent. We had a couple drivers, and two care takers for our home, and us kids (my brother and I) while my parents worked. I became extraordinarily close to Lena, a female pembantu. This meant that she lived with us, and was paid well, and was required to mind everything from making dinners, washing clothes, cleaning the house, minding the children, and assorted odds and ends. Despite her role to our family, she became part of our family. She and I spent countless hours together and we truly got to know one another. It was her that I ran to for comfort, or when excited about something. It was her that comforted me in bed when I could not sleep due to the fear that the bathroom cockroaches would get to me. And she was by far the most challenging individual for me to leave behind. I still remember the day when we were required to drive off and get on a plane back to the U.S. for a final time, and it was heart wrenching for us both. Lena was truly a mother to me in ways that cannot be expressed in words. She taught me right from wrong when I didn't want to hear it and fueled my interest in Indonesian culture by teaching me the language. I did the same in making an attempt to teach her small English words that she needed for around the house, and it was a bond we cherished. There was no pressure to conform to her Muslim faith, nor did I want her to become a Christian. Yet we could live together, love one another, and grow as individuals because of our open-mindedness towards learning new things instead of changing each other.

Anim, our male equivalent to Lena, was a little less tolerable of my attempts to be close, yet he was still just as pleasant to be around. Both would teach me how to cook traditional Indonesian foods and despite being too young to remember the recipe or methods of cooking, that memory is forever engrained in my brain. There is so much we can experience from each other, concepts to merge, so much so the possibilities are truly endless. Yet in this day and age, the idea that seems popular in everyone's mind is concurring. We need to dominate in order to value. Be it land, nature, culture, religion, or other humans. And it is a sad and depressing reality that will one-day result in our demise.

Chapter 3

A Few Rare Breeds

iPad games are the crack of the millennial generation. I swear some evil geniuses decided to band together and conjure up some fucked-up idea to make a non-drug related addiction to get people to buy into. Low and behold, the iPad was born. Not to mention, the smartphone which is the world's cruelest joke for people like me who grew up with record players, tape recorders and typewriters. I have to admit that in my weakest hour I too bought into this "smart" machine craze and now I find myself spending weeks on the same level in a game that I thought would be more entertaining and interesting than the last one. Only to find out two levels in that it is just the same game, with a different theme, and the levels are still as hard as the last game I gave up on after being bored since I could not move past one level. They suck you in and I swear another group of evil geniuses were sitting together plotting how to make these games addictive and require as much money be spent on the game as possible. For those of us who can't seem to get just 30 water drops and 35 red berries, this seems enticing. Because who wants to spend all day searching for a new game on their iPod, that mimics the last one, and has easier levels…just so long as you don't pass level 100. After level 100 you are doomed. Give up and move onto the next one.

I actually have a food game that I've gotten to over level 1000 on. I won't go into how much money I dropped in order to make that happen, but after investing so much time on it, I can't stomach hitting the delete button to get rid of the darn thing. It's almost like a hall of fame moment that I need to keep around just so that I can feel accomplished. Here I thought I was special in that I managed to achieve this, but if I bothered to compare my level to others' I'd quickly realize that my progress means jack squat. Because there is always someone who has invested more time, more energy, and more money than you. You will never be the top player. Don't kid yourself. So, here's this little cherry hanging over your head that's just out of reach, and yet somehow you find yourself seriously believing yourself capable of achieving fame and glory. Even if just for a few minutes or an hour, you reached the top spot. Then it's robbed from you, all while you were basking in the glow of success only you give two fucks about. No one else saw it, therefore there's not a bit of evidence. And since you're so consumed by your game on your little portable device there is no friend to acknowledge your success, because you have forgotten how to be face-to-face with someone, if you ever knew how to interact with people at all.

Yet somehow, it's a cycle I cannot rid myself of. I'm still trying to find a theme that suits my personality. I'm still trying to find a game that will have easy enough levels, that go past 100, so that I can just enjoy checking out for a while. Since I hide in my house regularly, (I need parental supervision in public) I need things to occupy my time. Write a book, someone said. Earn a master's degree another person said. Start documenting every waking hour of your life in a scrapbook for our imaginary offspring my husband said. Check, check, check. Now what? I have literally watched anything worth watching on my Spanish Netflix that has English audio or English subtitles, so yes, I'll get sucked into the world of iPod and iPpad games. I don't even know if there are iPod games, but it sounds good. Plus, it's part of the Apple community so I don't doubt that they do have games, I just haven't bothered to check.

I miss when things were simple. When you could walk down the street and not cringe when you saw another human being. Now I'm trying to analyze every waking second of my interactions with every person I see. Judgement written all up and down my face. I'm trying to ascertain their angle and figure out how they are trying to play me, or if they are sincere. Nevertheless, part of me - the angel side - tries to give everyone the benefit of the doubt and has some hope left in humanity. The other part - the devil - is slowly taking over. It believes after a series of trials and tribulations that people are no longer as honest as they used to be. For that, I need parental supervision. Usually in the form of a friend, because who in the world would want to look after a thirty-something year old human bean who has no filter and gets in more trouble than ever imaginable? A few rare breeds, that's who. Thanks to those folks I've managed to stay with my head above water, but once they leave my side, I know the safest place for me is behind closed doors. After all, who is going to visit my house? You better have an outstanding reason for knocking on my door. Be it you know I love you and wouldn't mind you bursting in unannounced and interrupting my nap time. Or you are willing to sacrifice yourself for the greater good, because that's inevitable.

When I come to the door looking like medusa, this is not the time to strike up conversations with me. No, I don't require coffee, but more than likely I have a migraine and whatever your selling isn't important enough to me at that moment to put your needs above mine. Not that I don't spend the majority of my time trying to give back to the community, but I just frankly don't find interest in a large group of friends. I find that keeping things close to the vest has the best success, and truly getting to know a person in and out by spending lots of waking hours with them, and some cuddle time, is best! Those are the ones you die for. Those are the ones that love every quirk in your handbook, and certainly wouldn't have you any other way - even when you know how to get under their skin, and you do it for fun!

A great friend of mind, named Kim, is lucky enough to have me in her life. I say that knowing that I am really the lucky one! We met the day I arrived in Rota, Spain with my suitcases in one hand, and my husband's in the other, with not a clue of what to do next. She had managed to show up on a whim, just in case extra people or luggage room was needed, and sure enough, she quickly became a steadfast friend. Throughout the day there was an exchange of excessively personal information – the kind you usually save for later, and a series of brash behaviors that led us to the conclusion that we were to be friends for life. Eventually, she lived down the road from me, and there were not many days we did not at least text each other. Most days we ran errands together, and on rare occasions we would experience so much more!

One fine morning she contacted me and said she needed to buy shoes for her teenage son who was caught with a hole in his shoe's toe. So, I met her at her house and as we were preparing to get into the car, I noticed she was intently staring at the old tennis shoes that she had in her hand (for who knows what reason). I was in a particularly amazing mood that day and had a moment of severe excitement over the notion that one of two things could happen. Kim could continue staring at the shoes, and eventually put them down, and life would go on. Or I would get to witness stupid! Sure enough, I got to witness stupid! I watched as Kim finished her few minutes of deep thought and concern over these shoes and progressed to slowly elevate them to her face and sniff inside them. Immediately regretting her decision, her face scrunched up and her head began to shake from side to side and I lost all military bearing. Tears started streaming down my

face as I laughed and said, "That's so stupid! Why would you do that?" over and over again. Kim did not feel this tragic sequence of events was nearly as funny, but there is not a day that goes by that I don't jokingly berate her for her actions that fine morning! Because in all honesty, that had just made my year!

This friendship was made of what people are rarely fortunate enough to witness, let alone experience. There was a loyalty there that would rival all others. A few other people in my life have connected with me in this fashion, but this was one for the storybooks! We would sit at military events together and I would whisper inappropriate or sarcastic comments under my breath to her and try to get her to laugh. There were other times I would try and break her, and get her to the point of no response, because there was always a response. Just a simple catch of the breath was what I was looking for and believe you me I got it! I would intentionally row Kim up just to see what she would do. And while I sat with a beaming smile on my face, she would look over and realize that I was intentionally poking the bear, just to see the end result. In the event she noticed my intentions I would then get the moment I was looking for. The short intake of air, and the quick exhale. A gloriously satisfying moment that happened all too often. At one point I figured she'd catch on, but she was never that lucky and I always walked away with my head held high!

Over time I spent lots of hours trying to make friendships work that were truly not worth having. There were violations of trust left and right, and the effort put in was not nearly as rewarding as the friendship itself. After I hit 26, I realized that life was just too short. There was no reason for me to be spending hours and hours on friendships that didn't matter. I began to remedy the situation. For a while I was stern and unwilling to befriend new people, and the popular misconception was that I was a snob. But anyone who knew me knew what I was doing and why. And they loved me for it. I was the bulldog that everyone had to pass by in order to get into my circle of friends.

Speaking of bulldogs (or more accurately, a bull in china shop), I met my husband in Devil's Elbow, Missouri at a place called The Elbow Inn. (I may have mentioned it already, if not I'll hit it again later.) It's located on historic Route 66 and is home to an amazing group of individuals. We were considered regulars there for a time, and though we were never extraordinarily close until we started dating, it was always a fun time to drink, flirt, and talk shit. If you were incapable of being able to do any of those three things you were the odd ball in the equation. Nevertheless, those who were considered regulars became a family, and before I knew what had hit me, I had returned and remained in the area for nearly six years. John and I started dating in 2014, and were married later that year, in the very bar we had met, by the owner of the bar. And watching our communities join was less than hysterical. He grew up in the outskirts of New Orleans, Louisiana, and I was the one who had hopped all over the globe. We managed to make a wonderful team. Through this union, however, I was unknowingly committing myself to participating in what John described as, the zombie apocalypse plan. To anyone who knows us knows this is a completely normal thing, but when I first discovered this, I soon realized exactly how serious my now husband was. He married me because I was capable of navigating on land, especially by night, and could therefore get him to Louisiana to pick up his best man and groomsman and we would rule the world together. I wish I could say that this was the least abnormal plan in the world, but it made sense, sort of. Until I was told that I would repopulate the country, at which point I realized that I needed to get another female on board, because there was NO way I was doing all that to myself! Not that I don't love kids, but three men, one woman. You can figure out exactly how uncomfortable any respectable chick would be with those odds. Not to mention the wear and tear on the human body after one pregnancy, let alone an entire football team, which seemed to be John's goal. So, I slyly suggested we find someone else to join us, because we didn't want inbred grandchildren. It worked! One of the guys married a chick so now I don't have to bear the weight on my own, pun intended!

The greatest thing about a union is moving in with each other! Like most females, I am particular about the way things are around my house. Unfortunately, so is my husband. We both knew that there would be something that we would go head-to-head over. For me, I didn't think it could ever get as low as a fork drawer. But, as luck would have it, silverware it was! My husband possessed a rather heavy set of silverware, since he is after all way stronger than I. Back then, I possessed a lighter type of silverware, and I did not see the use in combining the two, because what would happen if I couldn't find a light spoon amongst all the heavy ones. Right? Wrong. My husband kept fighting with me about combining the two sets into one drawer, but since we had an extra drawer, it only made sense to keep them separate. That way, he could use his, and I could use mine. Before we got to the point of knock down drag out fighting, I finally admitted that it made no sense, but my obsessive-compulsive tendencies were not going to give way on this one. Eventually we opted to let me win this one, and the fork drawers stayed separated. When we finally got to Spain, we compromised with a new set, sold the old ones and bob's your uncle. Problem solved.

At our wedding a few people brought us gifts, which was unexpected. The only gifts we really wanted was the company of our friends throughout the night. Nevertheless, we opened the presents the day after our wedding, when we were still intoxicated. This was a master plan of epic proportion. One couple had gifted us a pair of nerf guns, with a card that read, "There is nothing you can't solve with these." Perfect, right? In our drunken stupor we thought it was hilarious, and brilliant, because it was. It was brilliant right up until the moment I returned home from work and caught a nerf dart between the eyes. That was less than amazing. I could have been shot anywhere else on the body, but no between the eyebrows it was. And while it did not hurt, it definitely shocked me and turned me mad. Mad as hell. So mad, in fact, that I continued into the home and found my air soft gun, and when my husband least expected it, I pelted him on the elbow with my airsoft 9mm. Of course, he thought that was worse than getting hit between the eyes with a nerf gun, but as we talked through our respective experiences, we soon agreed that we were probably safer not firing either weapon in the confines of our home.

I think a lot can be said for the choices you make over the course of your lifetime. A lot can also be said for the type of people one decides to surround themselves with. For me, this became a no-brainer. Hang out with the people that will tolerate your crazy and everything will go as it should. I feel as though if it were anyone else saying this, there would be eyes rolling. Crazy, like misery, loves company. But it is the type of crazy that one must seek to perfect and find in others. There are more variations of crazy than there are hair colors, it would seem. Therefore, it is essential to find a compatible match. For example, one who does not take things too seriously is never going to get alone with someone who takes everything seriously and flips out because of it. That may seem like rocket science to some, but it is one of the hardest things in life to understand. And most people fuck it up.

Chapter 4

Deadly Commitment

There is a degree of uncertainty when one marries someone. I waited 29 years before getting married for a reason. I knew what I wanted out of life, or at least I like to think I did. I wanted a chance at a career, and if the situation involved another person, then great! If I didn't find anyone worth settling down with by then, well, I would just continue as before with work as my priority. But by the time I was in my mid 20s, my body and mind started to play tricks on me. My mind told me that I was lonely, and by night it would torture me with dreams of pregnancy, babies, and kids. Nevertheless, there's something to be said for the guy who enjoys a strong woman, which I was lucky enough to find in John. There is no pressure to be something I don't want to be. Although he encourages me to improve myself, there is an avid understanding that I am my own person and will make changes as I see fit. And I see him as a grown-ass man, capable of doing whatever he wants, provided he's willing to pay the price for it. And that's our reality. It reduces a burden that marriage puts on many. We coexist and are great friends. And this used to be the mentality back in the day, to have a spouse who you knew in and out, and who you loved to spend time with. Versus a virtual stranger you hopped into bed with. As much as I love my husband, there are moments in anyone's life where you can't stand that person. You may love them, but you can't stand them! This happens to me every so often, when I climb into bed thinking I'll get some sleep, and quickly realize I have a snowball's chance in hell at making that happen.

As much as I love my husband, for all his strengths and weaknesses, I am convinced he is hell bound to end my existence by night. At some point, some idiot decided it was a fantastic idea to legalize the union of two people, until death do us part. And to make matters worse, they tied religion into it, which guilt trips the fuck out of people who realize after the fact that reality may not be as amazing as they originally thought. My husband waited until after our union to expose the true nature of his restful insanity. Courtesy of restless leg syndrome and sleep apnea, every night is a saga. That being said, I think there is also some unconscious pleasure on his part that is achieved the following day when he wakes, and I fill him in on the happenings of the night before. Some nights I will walk in, and my side of the bed will be relatively untouched, and my husband's legs and feet will be in the air (while sleeping on his stomach, or on his back). Other nights I'll walk in, and he has got himself diagonally across the bed, and then other times he's cuddled up with the California king sized comforter, as if it's a body pillow. At times he's actually handed me a corner of the blanket, as if to say, "here you go love," but a corner does fuck all for those who don't want to freeze. Since my husband is a big man, he cannot get his body temperature down if the house is 70 degrees or above. I have actually gone so far as to bring an extra blanket into bed with me, and a few minutes later he will pull the extra blanket on top of him, because he is cold. Leaving me with absolutely nothing left to do other than sleep on the couch.

One night stands out above most others, and this night I walk in and think, "oh great! Maybe I'll actually live through tonight!" Worst mistake ever. It was a trap. A horrid, horrid trap. The bed was relatively untouched, John was sleeping straight on his side, and my pillows were unmoved. And as I lay down, I wondered what would be the drama tonight. As I fell asleep, I slipped peacefully off into my own head, and was later abruptly awoke by the inability to breathe. My husband's favorite pillow was on my face, being held down by the weight of his arm. As a man over six foot, weighing close to two hundred and forty pounds, this arm is heavy. More so when it's dead weight. So, I grab the pillow and move it (and his arm) into a comfy spot at his side and proceed to make an attempt to sleep again. And right as I drift back to sleep here comes the pillowed arm once again, on my face. Keep in mind, only certain men have "favorite pillows," and my husband is one such individual. So, I move the pillow (and the arm) to the same spot and whisper sweetly that I'm in bed, thinking that he will hear me and that will matter. And before I can fall asleep, yet again, the pillow returns to seal my fate. So, a bit more irritated, I move the pillow to a different spot, on the other side of him, and his hand let go. And if this dude did not roll over on his side, in his sleep mind you, grab the pillow and then roll back on his back to put the pillow down on the same face he had just tried to smother twice in a row. So, at this point, I've reached the uncool wife stage, one who does not appreciate being smothered in her sleep. And I'm fairly certain my husband has got to be fucking with me. So, I grab the pillow again, and put it on the other side of me, while talking to my husband about how he is trying to smother me. He responds to me, in a fit of rage, and starts arguing with me about how he is NOT trying to smother me, and he tells me to quit bothering him.

At this point in our marriage, I've learned that John has conversations in his sleep that he has no recollections of. And he does things that he never realizes he's doing, because he sleeps like a log. So, it occurs to me that this man will not have a clue what has transpired until I tell him about it the next day. And as sure as my natural hair color has changed over the years, he was completely oblivious to my trauma, caused at his hand. When I told him about it, he started laughing, and then quickly responded with, "I just don't understand why you don't appreciate that I love you to death." 100 percent dead serious. It rendered me completely incapable of speech. I shook my head and said, "I don't think that's the way it works." And this is one of the reasons why I love-hate my husband, because in an instant where you might not be pleased with him, he comes out of left field with some random comment or request that makes you reevaluate the entire situation. I would not be surprised, at all, if this was purely planned in advance of marriage, to torture me by night, claim he never remembers what he says in his sleep and has had conversations with people, just so that he can watch me spin out of control. I almost wish that was the case, because then I would be able to fall asleep quicker at night, instead of fearing for my life. Deep down, in the event all of this were made up, I would feel secure in knowing that my husband would not take it to the point of death. That he would be aware of what's going on, so if I stopped breathing, he would not continue his reign of terror. Unfortunately, this is as far from my reality as possible. For I am doomed to fall that the hands of a sleeping man, who loves me to death.

Other nights are relatively calm, aside from being kicked, catching a fist or two that's coming straight down onto my face (luckily, I woke up seconds beforehand), or moments where he decides I do not need my one pillow underneath my head. There was one such occasion when we first started sleeping in the same bed, where he literally stole my pillow from under my head while both of us were in a dead sleep, in order to use it to cuddle. I looked over at him when I recovered from the trauma of being woke up by my head slamming on the mattress, and he had this wickedly innocent and comforting grin on his face. The reason, I have no idea, but since he loves to harass me and steal my warmth, I can only assume it is simply because my head had been keeping it warm for him. Another night my husband decidedly saved me from a snake in his bad dream. This is the only time I have ever had the blessing of confronting him while he was conscious, in the middle of the night. The veracity he used indeed woke him up, and he could not stop apologizing to me for slamming his hands and fists on the mattress as hard as he could. The only catch, was one arm and one leg came down on my back and leg respectively. I must say that is true dedication to an individual. To sleep next to him years later and still know that you are lucky to wake each and every morning. Fortunately for me, no more snakes have tried to kill me since then. But I was completely unprepared for the violence and vigor for which he was willing to utilize in order to save my life from a dream.

There are other times, when I realize that I will have to kick his ass one of these days for doing stupid shit on my behalf. We were walking across the parking lot from our apartment in Missouri, when a car sped around the corner really fast. And I shit you not, this man started approaching the car, bucked up his chest, and was like, "You will die before you hit my wife." Don't get me wrong, I'm not unappreciative of the sentiment involved with that act, but as the car stopped and John came back to me, I was livid. Because the care could have put him in the hospital, or worse I would have to kill him myself, for his stupidity. Anyone knows that two people taking the brunt force of a speeding car is much more likely to result in survival of both parties. In all honesty, I have no fucking clue if that is remotely legitimate, but it sounds good. And it would save me from having to cause damage to a hospitalized man or haunt a dead man for his inappropriate use of chivalry.

Nevertheless, despite these " little" things that seem to test a marriage, we have both managed to enjoy each other's company thus far. We have both been put through so much that our motto is to enjoy life, rather than stress over the little things. Huh, ironic! We joke around constantly and very rarely ever get into arguing matches and that boils down to what I can only describe as respect. Not the new version of respect that everyone throws in the face of people they're in an argument with. But true respect, that anything we spat about is not more important than our union and love for each other. In this day and age, many folks get married without understanding what it takes for a relationship to last. You need support, friendship, encouragement, and a solid level of commitment. The commitment means, not stepping out for emotional or physical affairs with others. Truthfully, that was our one rule. If we got sick of each other, God forbid, that we would break things off before doing anything with anyone else, out of respect. We hold no disillusions about whether or not it is realistic to think that two people can stay together for life. But we take it a day at a time. And value the little things.

Another interesting point that I think people fail to understand is that blaming someone for something that has happened is never beneficial. If you are upset because something traumatic has happened, be it a car accident or God forbid the death of a child, antagonizing each other when you need each other most will only render you bitter and alone. Placing guilt and blame on another individual for acts that may or may not have been his or her fault is toxic. And while I have never been through some of these things, I have been through significant circumstances where I could have been blamed, yet my husband chose not to. It helped make us stronger, as we healed in our different ways, and it strengthened our marriage and tolerance for the other person when they act a fool. 2016 was where all hope went to die. From early February on through the end of November we faced hit after hit after hit. And through it all we knew we had each other. While our coping mechanisms are different, and we express our feelings quite differently, we knew it didn't matter. Because at the end of the day, we had each other to count on. That undying devotion, if you will, to make this thing work. We experienced a couple cancer scares, a terminal diagnosis of a close family member, a miscarriage that required surgery, surgery complications that rendered me anemic, and finally, the death of the terminal family member. It was incredible. I have never experienced a peaceful union throughout so much turmoil. We literally could not catch a break, because every time we had a hint of hope, it was followed up a few hours or days later with more bad news. And by the end of the year the only thing I had left to live for was my husband, and the fact that I had others that depended on me. Oh, and I was completing my final course of my master's degree in Criminology which required me to complete my thesis in three weeks, instead of eight. That was a gem! It did, however, afford me the opportunity to get my mind off things, and remind me that I could be way worse. My focus revolved on terrorism, because I'm special and like messed up minds. I knew families had experienced devastating losses all at once or had to live with regular violence and bombings in their communities. I also realized that I could very possibly be Muslim myself, and be hated for the actions of others, just by the mere sight of me.

By the end of the year, and the start of a new one, we were in Venice, Italy together celebrating the strike of the clock, and had hoped that 2017 would bring in more joy and hopeful times. Throughout the majority of this year that has been exactly what we have experienced, minus another cancer situation. Because why the hell not! This silence gave me and him both time to reflect on the occurrences of the year prior, since we were constantly in survival mode. For the first few months I was doing really well, and then everything hit me. Throughout my crazy period, I managed to never have to worry about whether or not I was a burden on my husband. Because with a few updates every so often, he would just tell me that he loved me, or send me a little something on Facebook or over email to make me feel better about myself. And that is support that you cannot live without. My husband said when we first talked about marriage, "I need a ride or die bitch."

The real moral to the story of life and marriage is this: there will always be a moment when the tides turn. Not necessarily in your favor, mind you, but they will turn! Karma came back to bite my husband in the rear. In one week, my PTSD diagnosis came full speed ahead and on three separate occasions, survival of the fittest kicked in something fierce in the middle of the night. This time, it was John, and the cat, who were lucky to survive. On a Tuesday (let's say), I nearly strangled the cat to death. I grabbed her by the throat with one hand and squeezed until she wiggled viciously enough for me to wake up and release her. Two nights later I pinned my husband's arm down, hoisted myself up and was getting ready to punch him in the face when he woke me up. The following night, I woke myself up just as I was grabbing onto his arm, braced for another attack. Since that week I have had a series of interesting outbursts, from evil laughter to slamming fists in the mattress. One thing is certain though, John stopped trying to beat me up in the middle of the night as soon as I started fighting back! Our friends have provided us with the perspective that at this point sleeping in separate beds is probably our only chance of survival. John says that's not an option, and I'm convinced living dangerously is the only way to go out strong! I guess time will tell!

Chapter 5

Orangutans & Penguins

There is legitimately no place in this world for people who cannot enjoy the smaller pleasures in life, in my opinion. Orangutans and penguins are these smaller things for me. Aside from the obvious enjoyment in a pet's antics, or the stupid shit people get caught doing by accident, penguins are by far the most incredible nature-born entertainment! Between their waddle for a walk, or their smooth slide on the ice, or their ability to swim figure eights in a pond, they are truly indescribable. And one fine day in Missouri I had this revelation. I had gone to the zoo in Saint Louis and witnessed something amazing! All three things were occurring simultaneously in the penguin pen at the zoo that day. And even though it was a short walk through the exhibit I left feeling inspired and motivated by these little furry creatures. There were some that were swimming figure eights, waddling from side to side of the exhibit, and more that were on their bellies using their tiny penguin flippers to push them forward and backward. They were able to make the best of their confinement by losing their ever-loving minds, and I was alright with that. And that was basically how I began living my life from that point on. My sense of humor began to get drier, my skepticism grew, and my ability to laugh at the little things instead of freak out over them increased substantially. I had realized that life was truly too short.

I went down to the Elbow Inn that night and was severely ridiculed by friends for being so excited over penguins; it occurred to me that I would have to stand my ground. I continued to offer argument after argument as to why penguins were awesome and before I knew it, I was mad inside. Mad that no one took me seriously, so I charged, penguin style, at my friend, and attacked her with my chest. The guy I was seeing at the time, said, "Oh my god, it's the Jennguin!" and from that moment onwards, that was how I was known. The girl named Jenn who loved penguins. But tell me honestly, have you ever seen a sad penguin?

Since then, I have maintained the nickname, and my fast appreciation for the little arctic creatures, and I've even been scarred by Kim sending me pictures of penguin-fish, instead of goldfish, that they have devoured. Or little gummy penguins another friend found and purchased for me, which I refuse to eat for fear that I will like them too much. Or the fact that one day my husband suggested we start to get rid of some of the crap we didn't need in the house, like my plastic penguin collection. No joke, I thought, surely he's kidding, and as I came to realize he was serious my heart broke a bit inside. I quickly gathered up my collection and hid them from myself, so that he would not find them, and the penguins would be saved. Even to this day, a few years later, I still have no idea where I put them.

Orangutans, on the other hand, are amazing! They are crazy little furbots as orphans, and these huge monstrous creatures when older. Yet they carry with them a wisdom that other apes don't possess. It is my perception that chimpanzees are brutal and aggressive little shits, and silver backs are the intimidating masters of their race. But orangutans move slowly, purposefully, and do not have a violent bone in their body, or at the very least, I have yet to witness it. When I was younger living in Indonesia, we did an orangawalk in my school, where we raised money for the growing population of orphaned orangutans. We even got to go visit the zoo's orphaned orangutans, and as I walked into this closed off exhibit I was swarmed by these creatures. They climbed me as if I was a tree. I had two in each arm, one on my head, one on my waist, and one on my leg. All at one time. No other kid in my class was covered as I was. And all I had done was stand there. They came off their little playground and decided that I was the next tree to climb. And sure enough, after we had spent some time there, leaving them was the most difficult thing I had to do.

My desire to return to these fuzzy little creatures got so bad that I was going to go live in the middle of the Indonesian jungle and work alongside other caretakers and be one with nature. Seeing as my college days were spent as a hippy/athlete (weird combo, I know) I embraced the idea of re-learning the language that I once spoke rather well, and reliving what it meant to live in the middle of nowhere, since that has always been my dream. I need no computer, no internet, no cell phone in order to function. I also need very few visitors, a short list of approved personnel, granted permission to venture out into the deep dark depths of my forever home. But the thing that most enticed me about doing this job was the opportunity to get back to a respectful environment, to learn about how to improve the quality of life and advocate for a being that is slowly being eliminated the more rain-forests are destroyed.

– *Chapter 6* –

Extenuating Circumstances

If you have ever become a regular at a biker bar you know there are always certain times of the day when the same people show up. As it happened, I was one of such people that liked to randomly show up and visit with all the walks of life. There were the retirees during the day, in the mid to late evening there was another crew of elderly folk that would show up, and in the nighttime all things young and spry would pop on through. But my joy of the place was never about being around people my own age. I've been described as an old soul, by the doc mentioned earlier, which basically means I was born in the wrong time period. That's my version of interpretation though. (I didn't like doc's view, so I quickly forgot it after fighting to prove his definition was just plain wrong and insulting.) Nevertheless, there were always a group of silver haired gentlemen who were veterans, that would be a little over the top with their comments and gestures. I want to call them pervs, but that just sounds insulting, because in all truth, there was a loving flirtation there. But I would wear holy jeans and a tank or t-shirt, and they would stick their fingers in one of the holes when I wasn't paying enough attention to them, and since I'm more conservative with my choice of clothing, the holes were never anywhere offensive. Maybe around the lower thigh or knee area. So, there was a level of almost-creep present, but it took a while to get our friendship to the point where that was completely normal.

The group of us would sit around and chat about our days in service or theoretical stuff about the way the world was going to shit, and occasionally we would play some pool. Now, mind you, this was a trap. Very seldom did anyone wish to play pool against me because the one table present in the Elbow had a particular slant, and it was MY table. No ifs, ands or buts. So, someone might float in that we didn't recognize or that would be a visiting relative of one of the regulars and they would set the trap to have someone put quarters down. Well, seeing as I was a daily player back then I would watch others play, in order to learn, or to assess talent. More often than not, that paid off. My goal was never to win outright and insult someone, more so it was my intent to enjoy the game and play to a level that didn't make the other individual feel uncomfortable. Every once in a while, you would see this poor sop think he was the shit at the game, and carry an ego with himself, and then get slaughtered. Usually by the hands of a female. That in and of itself carried a certain sting to it, because not many females are interested in playing pool. But the tomboy of my youth refuses to let me engage in karaoke or sit around and talk about makeup, boys, or gossip. So, I remained relatively independent, and played pool. There is nothing more insulting than a guy looking you up and down, and assuming you cannot play pool. That gets me fired up inside in a way that warrants vengeance. In those circumstances, watch out. Because I will show no mercy. But it was a great way to flirt, back in my single days, and it was a great way to strike up conversations with people about their talents, their lives, or their reason for being down in the middle of butt-fuck nowhere. We had quite a variety of people that would show up on any given day, because the place was located on Historic Route 66, which drew many foreigners who would spend their time riding their motorcycles from one point to another, along the route. It became a family affair. The female bartenders and I would have our own particular strengths like karaoke, pool, or other characteristics that drew people in and at any given time everyone knew to expect us to be present on a weekend. We would have a ball!

Some nights there was never a shortage of people purchasing rounds amongst the regulars. In fact, at points it got so bad that people were napping in their cars after drinking all day and night (well, namely me), or would do some far-out craziness that no one ever expected. A guy that I used to date had this little dog that loved to play with me. One night both came into the place, and before I knew it, I was on all fours crawling around on the bar floor with the dog. Everyone thought it was hysterical. Another night, in the middle of summer, I decided I wanted to make gravel angels in the parking lot. It did not work as planned, to say the least. There was no remanence of me having been there, and the level of disappointment was significant. Other nights, when only a few souls ventured out (during winter, for example), we would just enjoy each other's company and get crazy amongst friends. That was how I spent a good part of my 20s.

That was also when reality started to hit, and I realized the hard way that hangovers were a real thing. As time wore on, I felt more and more miserable, and some genius friend of mine decided that the only way I would feel better is if I had a beer the next morning. Meaning, come down to the bar at 10:30 am and keep me company because I'm lonely. And the cycle would repeat itself. Because after a certain point, you no longer feel the excessive alcohol damage in your blood stream. After a while you keep drinking, but never feel any different because you are just so messed up. There were friend or family gatherings that would take place that only certain folks were invited to. Any excuse to have a great time and enjoy each other's company was what we lived for. In the middle of the Missouri hills, what else did we have to do with ourselves? But it was that comradery, that trust that was built over the years of being there that always makes me feel like I'll be at home, whenever I return.

So, my husband. God love him! This special breed of a man decided that he was going to ask me out after seeing me down in our local hideaway repeatedly. Both of us frequented the bar and always liked each other, but for one reason or another - mainly just me being me - we had never gotten around to seeing each other outside of the Elbow. Fast-forward a whopping three years and a few rejections later, and we finally ran into each other again after a short period of not seeing one another. I had been working weekends, so I never went out, but my work schedule changed and then, magic. What was supposed to be a simple exchange of niceties turned wrong quite quickly. He was tipsy. I was relatively sober. And things started out well. From here, the story varies depending upon who tells it. But at least that much we agree on. My version, as only I can write, continues on like this - we were catching up, discussed how we were not seeing anyone else, and agreed to exchange numbers and go on a date. We also discussed how neither of us wanted anything serious, and as the conversation continued and John was mid-sentence he walked away. Disappeared. Went to go take a shot with a group of people. At which point I realized he would be back and didn't think much of it. When he did come round again, I explained what he had done and he just started laughing and said something to the effect of, "well, I had to go take a shot." As if that's something that justifies his actions. Nevertheless, I told him I was getting ready to leave and he started to say goodbye. It occurred to me that we had not exchanged numbers and he had forgotten about it, so I pushed him up against the wall and let him know I didn't play like that. Either he was serious about getting my number or not. There was not going to be some bullshit games and that if he really wanted my number, he was going to take it. I really didn't mean push him quite as hard as I did, which I recognized at the time. And I sort of expected a not so pleasant reaction. Instead, he started laughing. My head cocked to the side in a knee-jerk sort of reaction, and inside I thought this dude has potential. Sick, I know. But instead of someone getting butt hurt, it was curious that there was laughter involved. So, I let him down off the wall, we exchanged numbers, and from there nothing.

Nothing for a good few weeks. One day, while at work, my phone started to ring, and I looked down only to realize I had no idea who was calling. I kept saying the name over and over in my head trying to figure out why I would save someone's name in my phone and not remember. I was not in the habit of putting people's numbers in my phone with names, if I met them at a bar. Usually, I would just put XXX as the name, or as a note. That way I knew it was bs. Or I would only put a first name but this time, two names popped up. First and Last. I was utterly confused.

So, after pondering over it for a while, and obviously not answering, I realized that I did know who it was. That it had been so long that too many things had transpired and that I would go on a date with this man just to see what his deal was. After all, who waits nearly two weeks before calling someone they've been trying to date for nearly three years! Incredible mystery, I know! I texted him and let him know I was at work, and from there we agreed to go on a date, and we set it for the end of the following week. Of course, it was Valentine's Day, which neither of us realized until much later, and soon we rescheduled because we didn't want to deal with the pressure of that fake holiday. We sat and talked, and three hours later a very pissed off waiter got almost no tip for his extensive lack of manners. I guess the idea that in the States you can sit down and have a meal that lasts that long is disrespectful and rude. But we were catching up and talking about things. Following dinner, we went down to the Elbow, where we had met, and I played pool, and we hung out some more and talked. Upon getting ready to leave there was an almost awkward situation where I went in to kiss on the cheek and he had bent down to grab something and somehow we ended up kissing on the lips. It was only awkward because that wasn't truly my intention, nor was it his. But to make things less traumatic, we went in for an additional, purposeful peck, and carried on with the night. He went to his place, I went to mine.

What was supposed to be a "friends with benefits" relationship, or something casual, ended up without the benefits. Before he and I knew what was going on, we actually felt something. Disgusting, I know. One date became two, and so on and so forth. About two weeks in he left and went down to Louisiana for Mardis Gras, and apparently announced his intentions to marry me as he walked in the door of his childhood friend's house. Of course, I was completely unaware of this until much later. Nevertheless, a few short months later, we were married. I guess when you know, you know. Now after almost four years, it still seems worthwhile. Our ceremony was at the bar that we met in, the owner of the bar officiated, and the bar tenders were in my side of the wedding party. John's two childhood friends came up from Louisiana, our parents and my grandmother joined us, and all our Elbow friends were there to share in the event. The bar catered for us, and we stayed there all night enjoying just another night at the Elbow Inn! It was as stress free and easy-going as I could have hoped. However, I will say that there were moments where even I freaked out about the idea of a wedding.

I have never been much for crowds, nor standing in a front of them. I have most certainly not wanted to do that and confess my love for someone. It was just never me. I like small groups. One on one interaction. So, my wedding was to be as close to that as possible. The fewer the better. While I invited some great friends of mine, I was happy when there was no need to create a seating chart, or a gift registry, or list of people to send thank you cards to. In fact, the first thing I did was ask the two bartenders to be my respective maid of honor and bridesmaid. After they said yes, they both told me I needed to pick out wedding colors. The notion of this was utterly confusing and distressing to me. Who needs wedding colors? What does that even mean? I need a dress, my groom, a few people, and a certified official. I don't want a wedding song, colors, or any of that other crap! In fact, I freaked out so badly about it, that John talked to both of those friends and told them to stop stressing me out about wedding colors. Since I only had a few months in between official proposal and ceremony, I didn't want to make a huge deal out of it. In my mind, it would just be local, fun, and low stress. I drove a couple hours to Springfield, MO to get a dress and I found another dress in two colors that I thought might look good on my side of the wedding party. So, I suggested it, and the ladies were up for it, and sooner than later we were all sitting together drinking wine and creating do-it-yourself wine bottles and other décor from Pinterest. This is where a woman's love for wine goes to die. I swore off wine and did not touch it for almost a year after that.

At first the idea of decorating wine bottles seemed like a great idea, but after spray painting a few bottles and then adding a layer of spray stick-em, and covering one or two in twine from head to toe, that idea soon became not so awesome. Having great company and a few glasses ourselves didn't hurt, but by the end of it we were all done. We managed to match the decorations with the colors of the dresses the two girls had picked up, and then I had wedding colors, décor, and a wedding dress! I was doing great! I coordinated catering with the Inn and before I knew it, I was quite confident that I did not have to do much else. And so, I didn't. I just had to survive everyone being together in the same area, my family visiting, and get a bit of color before I was required to wear white. So, I laid down in a tanning bed a few times a week and tried (and failed) to lay off sweets so that I could fit into the dress I had bought. For less than $100 I did really good! The ceremony went off without a hitch, and before I knew what was happening, I was alone in the back of a taxicab, apologizing to the driver for the behavior of four grown men who were making a fool of themselves in a gas station parking lot.

We had finished off the night still wanting to drink, so there were the men's side of the bridal party, a close friend of John's from work that lived in the same apartment complex, and me all piled into a cab. They decided to have the cab take us to the gas station so they could pick up some more alcohol, and as they all spilled out of every door imaginable, I stayed inside and just watched them. I explained to the driver that it was our wedding day, and that those were childhood friends acting a fool together, as one of them came out with a fifth of something and shattered it all over the pavement. As they all stood around bitching at each other, one went back in to grab another one, and we all got back into the cab. The cab driver congratulated us and drove us the rest of the way home. We all made it safely into our beds, after a bit longer, and that is as far as the story goes for now, anyways!

On a completely different note, I recently handled a multitude of crises involving Hurricane Irma. This thing was a monstrosity for anyone living overseas with relatives in Irma's pathway. Since the news just makes me angry and I refuse to watch it, I didn't even know about it until the day before it hit Florida. My husband told me that the world was going to shit, literally. I was just as confused as you are, because that can mean a lot of things. After I muttered a ridiculous and unmotivated "huh", he explained that el Nino was finally killing us off. Not really, but that's how I interpreted his words. Four hurricanes, he said. Four hurricanes all at once. And it happened at the beginning of what they call hurricane season. Your guess is as good as mine when it comes to what that means, there seems to be a season for everything now. Shit, holiday season no longer includes Thanksgiving, Christmas, and New Year's. It has been expanded, to my dismay, to incorporate Veteran's Day, Halloween, and Valentine's Day. If that's not your perception you are seriously misguided. There were advertisements for Christmas starting in the beginning of September this year! I'm like, "Hello! I still have a few months to go there, missy. Stop stressing me out! I don't need to know how awful a human being I am because I'm only giving people cards this year, three or four months earlier than what is socially acceptable in my world. Leave me in peace. I don't 'people' well!"

In any event, I soon realized that nature was finally giving us a taste of our own medicine. Hey, we fail to give back to her, she's going to tell us how she feels. We have expanded our population to ungodly numbers and have way so many monstrous cities that it's hard to find a quiet piece of natural acreage anywhere in the world; guess what, she will retaliate. After all, she's been around considerably longer than we have. And she's a woman after my own heart about it, too! She sits quietly and waits. She waits patiently to see if you are ever going to realize that you are abusing her, and then finally, when you least expect it, shehe strikes. And she demolishes. That's my aim in life. I give everyone a chance, until they prove themselves unworthy. Then God help us all. There is no room for wrath in my world, but I remember. I will remember what happens, and I am an open book. As transparent and honest to a fault. So, when I tell people about my story, guess what...you will be in there at some point. And boy, have I met a LOT of crazy!

Anyways, back to the point...when I did finally get around to watching some of the coverage about Irma, I was very amused to find a public announcement from a local police force requesting that people not fire weapons at Irma. Well, that's just as genius as it sounds. I laughed to the point of crying over that one, because apparently that is exactly what kind of beings we have begun. I just envision someone saying "fuck it" after a few beers with friends, and going outside in their underwear and boots, nothing else, and firing off shotgun rounds at the sky. But it is stories like this that just make me think that maybe nature is right for giving us a taste of her medicine. There is truly no rationale for people's actions and for whatever its worth I have tried very hard to stop asking "why". There is simply no reason why. Yet, I keep finding myself grossly incapable of asking said question, no matter how much I try.

Speaking of crazy, which I mentioned earlier, I very rarely ever bond with shrinks, but there is one unique doc who I learned to appreciate, who would get down to seriousness, but also keep things light and fluffy. The witty banter back and forth, and the jibs that we would take made the dynamic extraordinarily rare. There was only one other doc that I valued, and there was a time I rotated offices every week practically. Regardless, this newer doc and I had been working together for a while to get my medications straightened out after another issue forced a med change. So, I did what any good patient would do, and started seeing another doc even though I hate the doctor's office. They never give you good news. Ever. But this guy was always a joy to be around. I would trash talk like the good ole days and not have to worry about whether or not anyone would give a fuck, because he was the department head at the clinic. (Yes, I have a knack for making friends in the right places!) Nevertheless, there was a few times I would go in and see him and tell him that I felt really unstable. He would shrug it off as just another thing, but there was a moment in time where I finally felt validated. To this day, he has never lived it down. He finally made a comment to me that he was displeased with how unstable I seemed. I immediately burst into laughter, and after seeing this guy for over a year, I basically screamed, "Where the fuck have you been? I've been telling you this for a while now!"He started laughing as well, realizing the situation, and from that point on I have been enjoying the pleasure of taking happy pills and normal people pills every morning.

On another occasion I was sitting in the waiting room for an appointment with our legal office when in came that same loveable doc. We said hello in our own unique fashion and I, after being up for about five hours already, by 9:30 am was feeling the coffee I had consumed earlier that morning. As I sat there jittering somehow our conversation shifted towards my request of my husband to make me a sound-proof box. This happened when we first moved to Spain, and sadly I have never gotten my box, but the theory behind it was, I would put my friends in it. Therefore, it needed chains, showers and a toilet. That way, if the Navy tried to steal any of my friends away from me, I could hide them. With or without their permission! To me, this seemed a completely reasonable notion. To others, especially my doc friend, it will probably lead to a special diagnosis from the latest DSM manual. I have never really been one for labels, though on occasion they do seem potentially useful, so in my boisterous manner, I told him I didn't much care for labels. He asked me what would happen when the police found out and came knocking on my door. I responded by telling him that I would simply explain I was protecting them and providing them with a support network. That the Navy moved us around too much and that it was for the safety and welfare of my friends that I would keep them by my side. It was also for the safety and welfare of the general public, because I require parental supervision 24/7. It has never been a great idea to leave me to my devices on my own, especially not in public. Much less, in a foreign country where apparently, appearances matter.

I will say that there have been times I've considered how simply life would be if I was locked away in some institution somewhere, and how much safer the planet would be. Just think about all the things you read here within this book and know that there is so much more that isn't divulged. With that in mind, what do you think? I think I'm extremely hard to kill. I think I'm the definition of resiliency because just when you knock me down, I pop back up. Usually, I have lost one more portion of my sanity, which I believe makes people socially acceptable. At what point do we have to call a spade a spade and put someone or something down for the sake of humanity? My husband and I have had this conversation many times before, with regards to the zombie apocalypse. If either of us are bitten, we will not hesitate to shoot each other in the head. It just makes sense, right? Would you want your current zombie, ex-lover walking around haunting your dreams? No, I highly doubt anyone would. So, put me out of my misery already, knock me up full of meds so I don't know what day, month or year it is (even though I'm honestly already there) and continue on. I promise you I will outlive all of you, even in that state! I am very hard to kill!

Chapter 7

A Calling

Since I was a young child, the only thing I wanted to do with my life was help other people. If anyone understood strife and chaos it was me, beginning from my pre-teen years and following alongside me throughout my older years as well. There were a multitude of low points for me, but the question I could never find an answer for was, "Why have I survived all this?" I was convinced that the only reason was to give back. To reshape my hateful teen years and start caring about people enough to make a difference in their world. Whether it be positive or negative, I don't always know, but my intent was just. I thought I would work forever in a youth care facility for at risk youth, and while I did do that for a time, it soon wore me down. The reality was that all these kids would come in and leave shortly after making progress. So, all we saw was the individuals who were struggling and at their lowest, most vulnerable, and spiteful. Although I did manage to get a lot out of the experience and heal personally, I quickly realized I had to leave. I could not take any more reminders of the things I had experienced in my childhood and life, not to mention I swore off having kids for at least two years following my departure. Nevertheless, I always sought out positions where I could assist those in need. I have always maintained a larger perspective of life, situations, and how various components of a circumstance play into one another. And I used that, and my conflict resolution or mediation background and certifications in order to help people get through those moments of desperation.

The true calling only came when I was committed to working as an unpaid volunteer for the government, as a Navy Command Ombudsman. Though this program has been around for a while, there are people within the Navy that still do not know exactly what that title means. So, after convincing my husband's Commander at that point that I had what it takes to be in the position, I was soon appointed. The job I agreed to take on was much more than I thought. I knew there was behind the scenes paperwork and administrative upkeep that was required, but never did I imagine spending 80-120 hours a month on other people. We (my counterpart, Oana and I) were put in charge of providing resource and referral information, managing communication between the command and the families and single sailors, enacting emergency preparedness plans, helping folks get through emergencies, and much, much more. We put in face time with the community to build a rapport, kind of like how police work is supposed to go and were available 24/7 to anyone who had a crisis. The program we received, during our transition, was not the best it could have been, to say the least. So Oana and I spent time revamping the entire program, and attempted to not only market the program, but market ourselves. And through the 18 months that I was fortunate enough to work with Oana we made a remarkable difference in our community. As I may have mentioned before, this is one of those things that kept me going, even when I was at my lowest. I knew people needed us, and I knew that I had to be available for others. So even when shit hit the fan, we maintained our professionalism, despite our every desire to throw the towel in, so to speak.

While we were a confidential source for our families and single sailors, we also had the opportunity to be apprised of various things that no single person should have to experience. Throughout the experience, I earned insight into what I was best at, and it quickly became a calling. I believed in what the program meant and was intended for, because I knew exactly how difficult it could be to arrive in a foreign country with my bags in one hand and my husband's hand in the other and ask, "What do we do now?" The response was, "I don't have a clue." For someone who had 21 years in service, and for his Army veteran wife that was a daunting concept. So understandably I realized that other individuals, with less experience with the military, might need a friendly face to show up and support them during a move across the globe. I began my involvement by sponsoring spouses, which meant I was in contact with them and would help them understand what to keep, throw away, or put in storage before their move. Then, I was to support them in the initial transition to a new environment. From that experience, I moved onto the Ombudsman position, which was a lot more intensive and required consistent knowledge of services available in the area, and how to properly utilize them to benefit anyone who might be in need. As a stay-at-home spouse, who only had her master's degree to focus on, this was an excellent way to guarantee I would get out of the house. And as much as I truly hate people (yes, I hate people) and prefer to be by myself in the comfort of my own home, this was a way for me to meet our community without actually having to befriend them.

I know that sounds weird and potentially insensitive, so let me elaborate. I hate people because of the evil that the majority of the world has grown to practice in their everyday lives. I'm not sure when it became socially acceptable to be an ass publicly but for some odd reason it has. Everyone is out for themselves, and the idea of community is now a concept restricted only to internet social groups. There is little time spent face to face with friends, and aside from those who use their phone for work related purposes, everyone spends the majority of their time interacting with their phone, while around individuals. It makes me question everything that people stand for. Whatever happened to playing in the streets, having one phone in the house (with the spin dial), that may or may not have been attached to an answering machine. You called once, if they didn't pick up, that was that. You knew they were busy, and you fucked off. I'll even go so far as to admit that we had a record player, I used tapes as a kid and even mixed a couple myself, and I used a typewriter! That is a forbidden commodity in this day and age. Somehow hiding behind a computer has given people the freedom to be brutal and to make assumptions, without actually caring to find out the whole story. I'm not sure if it is the millennial generation that I had been exposed to and hanging around so much that broke me, but they are brutal! Downright mean.

While I'm convinced that a lot of the labels, and peer pressure, and medical conditions are only partially justified, nothing validates your ability to be cruel to another individual. So, I prefer to have a small group of close friends, and to hide in my house whenever possible. With my pets, my husband (as long as he's awake), and occasionally have visitors. I've always been independent and never really needed interaction, but every now and again I get a buzz about me. So, one might ask, how does this tie into your unwillingness to make friends as an Ombdusman? The answer is simple: I'm willing to help people without confiding in them. I don't need to know who you are as a person, in order to be able to help you. Do I develop a rapport, and remember people's specific experiences, yes. That's what makes me great at this job, but do we have to hang out socially, no. There's a strict difference between my professionalism and my personal time. That may be harsh, but it is a requirement of the position, and it is the boundary that all individuals with a job should abide by. I have gone so far as to clarify whether or not I'm talking to someone as a friend, or Ombudsman, when interacting about a particular issue, so that they know that even as a friend I have certain boundaries I cannot violate. My job description and expectations of my boss require this. So even if someone is spending time with me as a friend, they are covered. They are capable of being themselves around me, yet simultaneously they know that there are some topics which the command must know about, and that is for the safety of everyone involved.

Though Oana and I have been praised repeatedly for our efforts and significant change we have created with this task, I continuously remind myself that I am just another individual who has experienced hurt, loss, and anxiety about the future. That regardless of what happens to the program after I leave, there will be an opportunity to aid someone else in understanding the nuances of the position. The point is to inform, listen, and to do what you can to reduce panic and uncertainty. Plain and simple, right? Wrong. Because there are moments when you will feel like a piece of shit for your efforts. There will be people that are never interested in what you have to say because they do not like you. There are people who will always hate you no matter what you offer them, because they are truly irate about their circumstances, rather than mad at you. So even while it is taxing to experience, at the end of the day it is well worth it. You get to physically witness the change in the community that you worked so hard to support. There is something to be said about the powerful impact a simple sincere "thank you" can have. Words are incredibly important, and how we relay each and every sentence can send an individual a completely unintended message.

Everyone deserves to give personal growth a chance. For me, that is through the multitude of experiences I have had in this position, while travelling, or while experiencing hostility (at the workplace, at home, or by a loved one). Learning what not to do is sometimes more powerful than what someone can teach you any other way. As strange as that may seem, I have learned what not to do my entire life, and yet things seem to be working out rather well. By all accounts on paper, I'm a successful individual. With bachelors and master's degrees, FBI certifications, Army Veteran, star athlete throughout college and high school, and a wide variety of professional experiences that makes me potentially marketable to any and all jobs. I'm hard working, driven, and dedicated to whatever task I embark upon, and yet there's something to be said about the opportunities you have had that do not appear on a resume. The quality of human being you are makes the world of difference, and impacts you in the employment industry, with friends, the opportunities provided to you from outside entities or family friends, etc. There is simply no way to replace an individual's generosity and willingness to grow. Be it by learning a new task with an open mind, by giving others a chance to prove themselves, or by allowing individuals to make mistakes without the severity of harsh punishment. That is the difference between the individuals who make great leaders, and the individuals who are toxic in their position of authority.

My military days have taught me all I need to know about toxic leadership. Mind you, I have had some amazing mentors, but I have also seen my share of individuals who are just brutal. They make the workplace demeaning, unworthy of your best effort, and downright awful to endure. It is those rare individuals that can inspire and motivate and make you a better human being. Chances are, you will be more capable of doing things outside your job parameters, and marketable for early promotions as well. My goal has always been to inspire. To engage in a comedic way that enables people to flock around me, or at the very least smile when they see me from afar. To be approached my someone with a smile on their face is breathtaking. It defeats this mentality that is found in younger generations where everyone is out for themselves, and perhaps this is just my way of encouraging positivity within the community I live in, and the world. Perhaps it's an effort to pay it forward, for all the times I was saved by someone's kindness. Or maybe it is just that I do not want to end up like the people I used to harbor hatred for. And the possibility that it's both is valid too! To have a job that truly influences your character, is enjoyable every day, does not fit the standard nine to five desk job for us free spirits, and can always be interesting and never what you expected is in every way my calling.

Chapter 8

How to Get Away with Murder

Taking the time to learn about how to concentrate on coping mechanisms instead of beating the living daylights out of (or killing) someone might be useful, especially in this day and age. Unbeknownst to me at the time, my undergraduate time in Northern Ireland would become quite handy later on in life. Learning about the history of conflict and violence there was enlightening, because I realized the United States was not the only fucked up country on the planet. In fact, I'm willing to bet that the notion of a great nation doesn't exist. Instead, you have a bunch of idiots raging about their own personal beliefs and opinions, which obviously collide with the opposing opinions. Before you know it, nothing has been solved, and everyone's up in arms about defending their personal beliefs. That is how I describe politics, at least. Nevertheless, while in Northern Ireland, I also was given the opportunity to take mediation courses and learn about conflict resolution from the ground level up. We worked as interns as neutral groups that were not affiliated with either side of the generations long dispute, and we took the time to engage with community members that were willing to put differences aside and recognize that similarities exist. For example, getting kids involved in after school programs can ensure generations from here on out see other individuals not for the political or religious affiliation, but instead as a person they had fun with. Parents engage in gardening or book clubs, and schools can perform meaningful plays, music performances, and other art forms in cohesion with other schools. Focusing on the environment was also a major distractor. This mimics the same thing I have mentioned before, why can't we all just get along and treat people well. You don't have to be a genius to realize that if we continue this way, we are doomed. We will kill each other, and the strength of every nation. The world is already at war with itself, over God knows how many issues, and no one benefits from any of this, except maybe the rich. They tend to benefit in conflict.

Getting away with murder is the act of allowing this domestic and international hatred to fester breed more. There comes a time when someone must put a stop to the discontent and stand up for the innocent children that will be raised in this environment and will more than likely spend years hating others all because the hate was present within the home they were raised. Yes, take a second to grasp that deep thought for a moment. After doing numerous research projects on the prison systems and the disenfranchisement that results in the American criminal justice system, I can honesty report back to you that one person being imprisoned affects many more than just that one individual. The family, both immediate and extended are affected within their social groups and having to cover down on bills and such. Families go from a twosalary household, potentially, to a onesalary household. With minimum wage what it is today, there is little to no chance for someone to work enough to pay the bills. Not to mention, if the confined spouse is lucky enough to be released within a decent time frame, who is going to hire them on? Although there are programs set up to foster their success, encourage education and technical skills, those programs are literally too sporadic to make a difference across the country. Housing will frequently kick prior confined persons out of their establishments, for fear that they did time, regardless of what their charge was. And there's little to no assistance for anyone that has broken the law because they lose the right to that when they caught and convicted of a criminal act.

Let's not forget children. Not only are they less supervised with one parent who is working all the time and another that is locked up, but they are also less likely to thrive positively. Research indicates that having a child experience an absent parent can lead to attitude problems and hopelessness, which affects them later on in life. Confusion about the role of the gendered parent that was absent could result in toxic relationships and let us not get started on that. Overall, the point is, we are failing our own citizens miserably, manifesting hate through multiple avenues, and failing to understand the role this will play one or two generations from now.

We simply do not possess the wherewithal to realize these things, and on a global civilian level, influence change in a nonaggressive manner. There are way too many protestors causing damage to their own communities and people of different beliefs to warrant any kind of peaceful protest or demonstration. That is what people used to do, gather peacefully. But now it has become acceptable to act a fool, damage your community, and expect the military's national guardsmen and women to help fix the chaos when the police are overburdened. I miss the days when you could talk about an issue that was different than another's views and be respected for it. That was the ideals behind why this nation and others were created. To allow certain things (such as dictators) to be prohibited. Yet, what we also fail to realize is that there are forces greater than our hatred for each other at work here. How many times do terrorist groups have to strike out at independent countries before we pool together resources, put our differences aside, and annihilate the major hate group of them all? I feel as though I need to point out that there is a considerable difference between Muslims and terrorists. One has contorted religious writings to fit political and personal agendas, while the other just wants to live a quiet life. There's also a difference between old religious interpretations, and newer interpretations. Just as the Bible was used to sanction stoning, burning at the stake, guillotine-like device usage, and many more techniques that have now been deemed inhumane. The same can be said for other religious texts, like the Qur'an. Another point needed to be made, is through time, interpretations of what is believed to be just or right, has changed. It is no longer appropriate to believe the word of one individual and send another to their death based upon that one person. We have trials, for whatever good they may do, to determine guilt. Following the guilty verdict, the consequence is handed down based upon the limitations posed by legal statues, and the circumstances of the person's character and crime. At least, that's my interpretation in an ideal justice system, but I'll get to that later, I assure you.

So how do we go from hating ourselves to focusing on the outside threat? How do we motivate people to understand that we are just as bad as the people waging war against anyone who doesn't believe in an extremist terrorist view? Because as we speak, terrorists are waging war not only against Westerners and foreigners, but also those within their own borders who refuse to adopt the extremist philosophy, which, mind you, is a cardinal sin in Islam. How do we deal with the worst of the worst, because as you will find out later, I used to be face to face with them on a day-to-day basis, and they have us pegged. They lure you in, and cause fear and chaos within your own country, and while you are distracted amongst yourselves, they hit sporadically and purposefully within the international community. Knowing that no one will shift focus outward, since so much internal chaos is occurring. So again, we are permitting people to get away with murder. Cold hearted calculated actions being followed through with time and time again, yet no one has decisively organized a group effort to force their exit from existence.

Since the cultivation of ISIS, the first group known to willingly kill other Muslims, there have been other groups that have developed within the same region, and neighboring regions (namely Africa). Greed is caused by what western countries deem high value, and as a result, terror wipes through entire nations. So, you tell me, am I crazy to think that this is going to lead to the apocalypse? The end all be all world war that no one survives. Because as of now, I'm still waiting for another 9-11. A thing that unites an entire country, rather than allowing petty bullshit to occur over things very few people still alive have even lived through. I'm still waiting for countries that are allies to pull together and spark an interest in getting rid of the groups that are willing to cause as much damage as humanly possible. Make no mistake, that is their intent. The extinction of anyone outside their belief system is their end game, and we are all disposable. So, unless you want those murders to be us, I would encourage our priorities change, quick fast and in a hurry. I suggest that international relations become more potent, meaning if you are allied with France, and if they get hit, you do something about it. An attack on my friend, is an attack on me. You want to weaken and destroy our ally, we will destroy you. And as I type this, I'm sitting in Spain, on a military installation. Barcelona was literally attacked less than a week ago, and yet the United States has done all but publicly admit they are devastated by the situation. Public acknowledgement of friendship and dedication does fuck all when going through the aftermath of an attack, and we are no longer living in a world where friendship means anything.

Chapter 9

Art as Inspiration

Many individuals reach out to music for inspiration. All art forms are generally used as such, yet music inspires the mood, the sentiment of someone's character, and has the potential to influence whether or not they are likely to pull themselves out of a terrible mood. It is used for celebration in collaboration with dance, and very seldom is there ever a ceremony of some sort, be it wedding, military function, etc., where music does not represent something. Take a first dance between husband or wife, for example. This carefully chosen song represents the connection between two individuals who have just signed their death warrant to each other. (I joke, but I truly do believe in the notions of unions.) Or, a military function that plays the National Anthem, or a sports game that does the same before the start of the game or match, etc. This represents something that the United States endured. Be it a moment of pride for some, hatred for others, each and every person interprets songs differently.

For me, I find inspiration in a variety of musicians. I enjoy hip hop, old school R&B & pop, jazz music, blues, country, and even classical music. I grew up listening to pop and what can now be considered old school R&B and pop during my pre-teen and teen years. I have developed a taste for jazz and blues following a few really outstanding movies I've seen. Country music is enjoyable because it relays the most hilarious adventures, revenge stories, and misadventures of all time. I used to play the piano, hence the attraction to classical. Hip hop, however, is a relatively newer thing for me, despite originally hearing it during my undergraduate years at Earlham, amongst my group of friends. Since then, I took a break from it while in the Army and hanging out backwoods Missouri for a while. Though I find one particular individual and one particular group intriguing, I love that hip hop touches the soul in a way I hope for this book. It is an eloquent play on words that discusses significant strife in life, that some individuals just do not understand. It is a message, loud and clear, to the listeners about things that really happen, yet many people ignore. Brother Ali, an Albino Muslim living in the United States, is one such individual. He inspires peace amongst brothers in his religion, and he is monumental for being proud of his appearance, who he is as a person, and the messages he relays to others. It is evident, by his multitude of albums, that he genuinely seeks a holy life. Whether or not that particular religious' persuasion matches up with you or me, I could care less. The point is, he has embodied what I believe religion intends to send as a message to followers. That is, peace. Be accepting of others that are not accepting to you. Be nice to those who are cruel to you. Have little to no hate in your heart, for it will wear you down. These things are apparent through his art form, hip hop.

Brother Ali is my individual artist I mentioned earlier. He has collaborated with my group of hip hop artists, Hilltop Hoods. These guys are Australian, and though the members of the group have changed over the course of their multitude of albums, they continue to inspire through upbeat tunes, that tell stories for each and every individual out there. They are a mix between sentiment, life exploration, good and bad relationships, and parenthood. What each concept means to these men is explained through their language and beats. The song they collaborated with Brother Ali on is a message about living and letting go. Ironically, it's titled, "Live and Let Go". Shocking I know. This song specifically addresses innocence and the lack of hatred in younger populations. That it is older age that generally makes people bitter, and spiteful. That the intent behind life is not to take crises and make them detrimental to yourself and others, but to test yourself and your ability to remain free from the burdens carried by so many. Those who refuse to allow themselves to give others a chance, will truly be worse off than those who choose to forgive and forget. That message in and of itself is extraordinarily powerful, considering the background of Brother Ali's religious affiliation.

I know I have mentioned this time and time again in my life, but hate will be the downfall of our species. Make no mistake, mother nature has had enough of us, but it will be hate that brings about war after war, which only brings destruction. Yet in today's society, the largest and scariest threat seems to be terrorists, who have contorted the Muslim faith and the Islamic lifestyle into something it does not aim to achieve. Brother Ali, working on a song discussing letting hatred go, could not be more ironic, in my opinion. Despite all that this world has said about people that share his faith, he chooses to rise above it all. Despite the levels to which fellow Muslims will reach to cause chaos, he has risen above their choices. The ability to do both is true wisdom being perpetuated through art, through music, and through hip hop.

The last artist that hits me where it hurts, so to speak, is a country artist. You may have heard of Carrie Underwood, and I'll be damned if she's not the most inspirational woman on the face of this planet! Taylor Swift may be receiving awards left and right, but it is Carrie Underwood who easily tops any dominant country music star these days. She has demonstrated her experiences through her lyrics. The fact that she was raised in a small town by religious parents, who encouraged her to succeed despite having to leave home. Carrie explicitly discusses real life scenarios people can understand on a personal level, be it affiliated with religious prayer, abusive situations, legal threats, unhappy circumstances we tell ourselves we deserve, loneliness, and more. These topics reach the hearts of every soul out there, because in some way they are relatable. Not to mention, these might be stories based on some degree of truth for Carrie, or maybe not, but regardless of the music she puts out for the public, she is capable of also recognizing that it is just a song. Though there may be people who are inflamed by a song or two on an album, Carrie is strong enough to recognize that not everyone will like everything she does, says, or performs.

Music can be inspirational, but it does not have to define you. I know many times I have felt sad, and I listen to songs that make me even more sad. It has effectively hindered my ability to move on and progress from whatever it is that I was sad about. Yet, simultaneously, music has all the power previously mentioned with regards to inspiring individuals and touching their hearts. The biggest misconception across the globe is that celebrities are someone inhuman. They are just as flawed as you and me, so singing about scenarios that involve revenge, or momentary weakness, is realistic. Yet simultaneously taboo. We have all been there. If you claim otherwise, I'd wager you were lying to yourself. Having someone step up and say things that ordinarily might be frowned upon, regardless of whether or not it a song, is someone definitely worth paying attention to, in my book.

Chapter 10

The Art of Resilience

This is a tale of how I got through my miscarriage, and the surgery that followed. For anyone who has lost a child they feel a certain level of grief. For a woman who loses a child while it is within, well that adds all sorts of other pain and anguish. Not only does it question your femininity by cultural standards, but it can cause significant pain which adds to the grief. I found out I was pregnant on the day or the day after I found out my tumor was benign. By that point in my cancer scare I no longer possessed the will to care about the results, simply because the process lasted three months. Thanks to living in Spain and having limited resources, and faulty machines and paperwork processes I had had enough. The pregnancy discovery was a relief, aside from the fact that I was not ready to be a mother, or so I thought. I had spent a lot of time prepping myself for this turn of events, and make no mistake the pregnancy was planned. After we discovered this revelation I went to an ultrasound appointment, which by the way could be very offensive, if a friend had not told me that the first one was done internally with a dildo looking thing. Imagine how many tears I cried over that one! Because it broke me. As did the notion of wearing breast pads, which the same friend also enlightened me about. I cried then too. They were not tears of joy. They were tears of utter disgust that I had to give up one pad a month, for two, on a daily basis. To say this did not sit well with me would be an understatement.

Nevertheless, the instrument for the initial ultrasound was rather inoffensive, to my surprise. I had pictured something way different, and I have no idea why. I guess in my time I have seen quite a few dildos (in shops and such), and planning for the worst is my strong suit. That way, if things positively surprise me, I can relax. Anyways, to get back on topic, I was experiencing the traditional situation with a friend in the room, above the hips. I was naked from the waist down. A male doctor (that I actually trusted) was placing the implement in and a female staff member was present. The fact that this chick survived was extraordinary. Once we discovered the heartbeat, she continuously made happy fluffy comments about me creating life, and how amazing it was. All I could think about was that I was naked from the waist down, my husband was at sea, I had a man other than my husband probing my insides with an ultrasound dildo, and my vagina had a heartbeat. Not only that, but doc had just told me he was going to be searching the cracks and crevices of my cervix to see if there was another one hiding in there somewhere. How big can that damn thing be? The last thing I was thinking about was the marvelous creation of life. I looked back at my friend and mouthed to her that this bitch was going to die. The only thing that stopped me from kicking her in the face was the respect I had for my doctor, and the instrument still inside me. And for the record, there is nothing okay with the idea that there are additional objects floating around such a tiny internal space, that could also have a heartbeat. I told the doc not to bother, because I was good with one heartbeat for now. He laughed, and continued his assessment of my situation, and relayed that there were no twins hiding. He removed the implement, and both the doctor and female staff member left the room to afford me the opportunity to get dressed. The chick handed me a box of tissues and as I looked at it, I was like how in the hell do I need an entire box of tissues to wipe off down there. What am I leaking out of some extra orifice I don't know about? Kim, my friend, immediately started laughing at how badly I wanted to end the female nurse, and the assorted other happenings of that few moments in time. Reality had just struck me across the face, and I was in shock.

Nesting became a popular pastime for me. As did research. I never had younger siblings, and I didn't experience much of the younger years of my cousins' lives, so I literally didn't have a clue what I was in for. Apparently, strollers of quality, which my mom-friends expressed I needed, cost 200 to 300 dollars! WTF? Why is that even necessary. Let's not get into how many diapers one needs to accumulate and the total cost of that, and of tiny baby carriers and sleeping equipment that I knew they would grow out of in months. So much money to be spent on something that would stay in it for literally, the equivalent of half a breath in time. Nevertheless, I created my list of things to acquire. Talked it over with the hubby and started preparing the house, meaning clean the third room we hadn't touched in over a year and a half of living in the same house. In order to prepare for this little terror that would cry, poop, sleep, and require me to feed it every two hours. I always knew I should have kids only when I was ready, and much older than the traditional high schooler (too wrong?), and I thought being thirty would be old enough. For that reality, no age is old enough.

Going from freedom to time constraints, two hours sleep intervals, and a gradual development of attitude was truly going to test my patience. Nevertheless, at some point I realized I was okay with it all, and that I was going to jump in, all in.

Well, I should have known better. After a while I realized that I was having a very easy pregnancy. That although my breasts hurt, I had no nausea or vomiting, and nothing else seemed to be happening. The doctor didn't think much of it either and just told me I was lucky. But soon I started to feel weird. I was short of breath, couldn't walk down a hallway I walked down multiple times, and I just felt lightheaded. I went in to do a checkup and talked to the doc about everything that I had been feeling. He told me that he would check out the baby, just to see what was going on, and then we would progress from there. He brought the handheld auditory sensor in and spent what felt like an hour searching for the heartbeat. After a few moments he suggested we get the other machine, to see what was going on, because the baby could have been in a strange position, and effectively hiding. Great, I thought. Either the kid already has personality, or this is headed nowhere positive. So, we went and did the external procedure and there was no heartbeat showing up, nor was there an image. At which point, knowing that I was supposed to be 13 weeks, and the doc looked a certain way where he was clearly trying to hide concern, that this was going to be a bad day. So, after the ultrasound dildo came out again, we confirmed that the heartbeat had stopped. After measuring it, doc told me that it had stopped beating on the day it turned 9 weeks. Meaning, I had been carrying my child for almost a full month without knowing of its situation. The doc told me that it was unusual that I didn't have cramping, and that since my body didn't flush everything out, I required surgery. This appointment occurred on a Friday, and by Monday I was in for surgery. Usually people catch this situation sooner, I was told, and they were very surprised that I had not shown symptoms earlier. So, into surgery I went. I was upset, yet trying to remain positive, because this was something that had to be done. No question.

After surgery, I woke up feeling amazing. I was transitioned into recovery, was given more drugs, and realized that I had a weird mesh diaper thingy on, and a catheter. The catheter was less than amazing. And every so often, when the medications started to wear off, I realized that I did not feel as amazing as I thought. They required me to stay around for observation because during the surgery I lost a liter and a half of blood. That's more than the average Nalgene water bottle, for those who don't know European measurements. I drink four or five of those a day, I have an unhealthy love affair with water. The surgeon eventually came in and told me everything, even though my husband had already told me. She said I was going to get home later that night, and everything would be fine, but they wanted to make sure my "levels" didn't drop too low, which meant I could need a transfusion. I said okay and before long I was starting to shift from pleasantly sweet patient to utter disaster, all because of my catheter. It had occurred to me that it was uncomfortable and messing with my medication high, and I wanted it out. I spent an hour and a half complaining about it, or so my husband would say, and finally someone came to remove it, a female nurse, with a male trainee. Poor guy's face turned red as he yanked the cord out and I expressed discontent with the situation. Before long I was assisted up and asked to go urinate, a million and one times, until there was no blood left to expel. The surgeon came back and told me that instead of leaving, I was going to have to stay overnight, and would be asked at some point to walk around the building repeatedly. I didn't like the sound of either of those things, but I took it in stride. I ended up walking 32 circles on the same floor, while talking shit the whole time. I realized after the fact that my robe was open in the back, so the staff got a pleasant picture of my mesh panties (waist high), and my rear. I could have cared less at that point though, and at some point, my husband got tired, so I stopped walking, too. We went back into the room, and as he was getting ready to get a few things in order, I quickly told him he was not to stay. Not with his sleep apnea and snoring. There was no way. I kicked him out after a goodbye or two, and then proceeded to try to fall asleep. With all the drugs in the world in my system, it was a wonder that sleep was the one thing I could not accomplish.

After watching Armed Forces Network (where television ads go to die) almost all night, I opted to try and sleep. I managed to get into a state of blissful rest but was awoken a few hours later with severe pain. I got into contact with the nurses and staff and requested medicine, which they had forgone to let me get some sleep. That was not a pleasant idea. Everything hurt. And as I waited for them to get the meds, and for the meds to kick in, I had one thought crossing my mind. I had no idea where my child had gone. I didn't know if I believed enough in heaven or hell, or angels, or Valhalla to know who was taking care of it, and where he or she was. Through the pain, the only thought I had was, this is the least I could do for a child that didn't deserve to not make it. The thought occurred to me that the pain that child went through was more than I ever could imagine. I started praying, for the first time in years, not for myself. But for my unborn child, for my husband who was devastated to lose his first child after waiting over two decades to have one, and who was shook up after seeing me in my state, post-surgery. To him I was superwoman, and superwoman was in a weakened state that he hated seeing me in. I also prayed for my friends, and everyone who had had a miscarriage before. I had been told that almost 80– to 90 percent of pregnancies end in miscarriage, yet no one seems to talk about this. As hard as it was for me to be in the OBGYN clinic after knowing I had miscarried, that did not seem relevant. I prayed for all those who would experience a miscarriage, or God forbid those who would survive multiple in a row. For me, that became a large fear. But most importantly, I knew I could get through this, because of my support system, but I knew there were others who would not be so lucky.

The next morning, they tested my blood levels and gave me the option for a transfusion, or to regrow my own blood supply. After being cautioned that a transfusion could complicate further pregnancies, I opted for the latter. Somehow, I missed a major factor in all this. By some means I left the hospital not realizing I was now anemic. My husband sat me on the couch like an invalid, and went into the kitchen to make food, and get me water. I was parched, like a fish out of water. I think it is a hospital's protocol to deprive you of the one thing you want the most, at all times. Anyways, a few minutes after sitting on the couch I realized I had to go to the bathroom. My husband noticed my shadow as I walked past the kitchen entrance and immediately asked me where I was headed to. I told him I had to use the bathroom and that I could do it. Nope. Boy was I wrong! I made it halfway down the hall before stopping, completely out of breath, and totally mystified. I had walked 32 circles around the hospital floor hours ago. Why could I not walk down my six or seven-foot hallway? I called to my husband and asked him why I couldn't get down the hallway. He replied by telling me that I had blood that was the consistency of ketchup running through my veins, and that is what anemia is and does. My reply, "Well this is bullshit! No one told me about this!". Apparently, I was wrong. Apparently, I had not only been told that I would need assistance, but that I would require help for the next few weeks. I was not okay with this. At all. As someone who usually does stuff for herself, this was not okay. My husband had to hold me in the shower. Eventually we put a waterproof seat there, so he didn't have to hold me all the time. He actually got tired of getting wet, which completely dumbfounded me. After all, he had not recently been knocked up, nor had he had a dildo inserted into his man parts, nor had his man parts had a vagina. Nevertheless, I could not get down the hallway or clean the house because it would exhaust me. My husband got to do the work since coming home to a dirty house was not ideal for him or me. Not that I was really going anywhere anyways. I felt bad watching him clean. If I tried, I'd get yelled at, and told to sit down. We had friends bring over meals, which helped tremendously, and some would stop in and throw insults my way knowing that I couldn't fight back. Those are the ones you know you love, because why else would you allow anyone to kick you while you're down? And gradually I started to become less feeble, more capable, and I about exploded when I got one chore completed in one day. That was a monumental moment in time. Soon thereafter my husband was suggesting getting me on a treadmill, and I scoffed at him. Bear in mind I don't work out. I'm not grossly overweight, but I'm overweight by about 20 pounds, if I'm underestimating. I don't work out. I am fluffy and I like it. And lazy. That is what the Army has done to me. All the 0430 wakeups for physical training was enough to cause my disinterest in anything athletic. I'll walk around, do errands, sweat when I'm doing housework, but you will never find me in a gym. So, for me, getting on a treadmill was asinine.

After about a month, I discovered I was cleared from my anemia diagnosis. I still wasn't even aware that I had anemia. I didn't know what it was called. I just knew it sucked and I now had a newfound respect for anyone with sickle cell anemia or just plain anemia. How can one live like that? Constantly needing assistance to do small tasks and requiring breaks because you feel your heart beating through your chest. That is a real thing. I have lived it. Luckily for us (sarcastic), the year was not over, because as soon as good news came, we were hit with yet another thing. So, while this situation was over, it would later resurface once I stopped living from one crisis to another.

Sometime during 2017 I felt a little unstable. I felt like I was really happy, and really unhappy. So much so that my husband, friends and doctor all noticed. I was put on "normal people meds" in order to help balance out my moods. I soon discovered it was because I felt shocked still that I had finally gotten on board with the whole having a kid thing, just as it was yanked from me. Throughout my recovery I was too concerned with trying to function to really have an opportunity to deal with the situation as it stood. To some degree, the medications they gave me post procedure had also messed with my brain a bit too. So, by the time I got to understand what 2016 really brought to me, I was close to losing my mind. I felt worthless at times. I felt ashamed. I felt like I had let myself down, even though there was nothing I did or didn't do that could have changed the outcome of my pregnancy. While that gave me some comfort, the only rationalization I had for why I would experience the gain and quick loss thereafter of a child, was to make me realize exactly how much I wanted it. Then came the feelings of sadness, because I don't do well with not getting my way. As I worked through my feelings with docs and friends, and occasionally my husband, I started to recognize unparalleled change within me. Clarity, if you will, about my circumstances, and where I could go from here. It never once occurred to me that I shouldn't try again, which seemed to be a popular question. I just needed time before all that happened. I needed time for my body to heal and repair itself, and I needed time before I could digest everything that I felt.

I have a curse. This curse is feeling every iota of pain and anguish that someone else can feel. When it happens to me, it sucks. Because the level of pain I feel is amplified by the fact that I know other people have survived these moments, yet I still struggle. It's a natural human process, but there are some things that I just can't get over until I have exhausted all potential emotions and concepts about a scenario. Had there been something I could have done to prevent this from happening, I'm sure there would still be random thoughts of doubt in my head. My saving grace, however, was that it was a nature survival of the fittest thing. That I had no blame to place on myself, despite still finding a way to place some level of guilt on my shoulders. By the time all was said and done with though, I know that I would never have traded that experience in for anything. It gave me clarity with where I was in my life. It provided me with hope for the future, and hope for the idea of molding someone into a good or great human being. Not necessarily by the monetary accomplishments, but by the character they possess within them. That became my focus for myself, as if I hadn't already spent years trying to do so. I wanted to continue spending time on myself, until I was lucky enough to have another go at parenthood. Until that happens, I will still be chugging along. I will be waiting to discover new ways to mold myself into a better human being for the more difficult experiences in life.

Chapter 11

Success Redefined

I accompanied my husband on the couch one day, while he was watching a documentary on Netflix. I had just woken from a nap and was too subdued to really care about what he was watching, but I soon found myself enthralled. It was a show about something called the Barkley Run, in backwoods Tennessee. This is a yearly competition that has been going on for years now, unbeknownst to the general population, and goes relatively unpublished. It is a run that you pay the organizer random things each year, in order to join in on the fun. They go through a relatively enthralling check in for candidates before approving them, to ensure the safety of the runners. The competition is grueling, to say the least. Encompassing a 100-mile adventure, under 60 hours, in the most brutal terrain imaginable. Since Tennessee has pretty significant hills in that area, there is elevation added to backwoods trekking that requires land navigation techniques, significant survival skills, and an amazing support system back at camp to help with the transitions between intervals. There are five twenty-mile circles, that start and end at the same spot. Usually, participants are lucky to finish one. In fact, 60% of the competitors are out of the race following the first round. 88% are done following the second circle. Most don't even make it through the second iteration, because they get lost, give up, sustain physical injuries, or are just plain exhausted.

The reason this competition is so highly sought after amongst certain hiker types is that there are literally a handful of individuals who have completed all five rounds. As of 2011, there were 11 people who had completed the course within the allotted time frame. 2012 was the year the documentary was publicized. That year was monumental in a lot of ways. Not only was it really the first time it had been published, to my knowledge, on an open forum, it rendered a successful completion of new heights. But there is much to tell before we get to that.

Throughout the race, people were positive. Using their peers for assistance with navigation, motivation, and sheer company. As the numbers started to return to the camp, there was a significant amount of comradery even between those who were not competing. The recognition that this was a significantly challenging experience was not lost on anyone present. As a tradition, when people would call it quits, one particular individual would play Taps on the bugle. As if to not add insult to injury, the song marked the end of the line for every participant who was accepted into the challenge. Good ole shit talking was also a very obvious pastime for many of the race organizers, who were at times brutal. That brutality fueled some, and most people appreciated it as a sense of motivation to defeat the obstacles ahead. Some were merely too tired to really care. Most participants who called it quits earlier on remained in the camp until the completion of the 60 hours, which I found enthralling.

As I mentioned before, there was no shortage of recognition about the endeavor every person there was embarking on. This bred a sort of ride or die mentality. That they were all in it together, no matter what. Their kindness and support to one another was expressed in a multitude of ways, sharing survival tips, fresh dry socks and other clothing, and by positive compliments and words of encouragement for those that remained committed to the self-destruction the course provided them. Another thing I noticed was that there was a recognition among everyone that the course itself was not necessarily about completing it. Yes, that would be great for everyone who put their time and energy into preparing for the course and running it. Yet, it was more about personal accomplishment for every soul there. Although some were disappointed that they didn't get farther, they could not be disappointed for long because they had embarked on a one-of-a-kind journey. Those who were running the course for the first time realized exactly what they were in for, and those who were considered veterans tested themselves by making it past the point they reached in previous years. Even those that were present in camp the entire time were complementary and shared special greetings for the incoming runners. The persons serving to set the course and organize the event would do the same. There were ways to ensure everyone had made it through every part of the course, so while checking them in they would take the time for progress reports, some compliments, as well as some words of discouragement, again to add insult to injury! It was clear that the challenges of the course were not only physical, but mental as well. Only the dumbest survivalists of them all managed to break through to the point of no return. Or so it would seem.

Sure enough, by the time the fifth round commenced, there were five competitors remaining. As they implemented new courses each year, with added special twists and turns to the way they run the race, they were now required to go in opposite directions. People who had been together since the start were now forced apart. To fend on their own, and to accomplish the almost impossible alone. As anyone can tell you, the last bit is the hardest part in any challenge, in some ways. This is when physical strife challenges the emotional capacity. Your body is worn down. You may or may not have slept in the last 48 hours, and if you have it was only for a short while because of the impending time limit. Delirium sets in. Mental warfare is a popular technique implemented in battle. This combination of things mimics that of any specialized branch training. To push yourself past your breaking point time and time again to build the knowledge and confidence in your survival is necessary for those considered elite. Though the motivations for every participant agreeing to continue through the fifth round may be unclear, there is a curiosity that provides. Maybe it is the sense of accomplishment that is the end-all, be-all goal. It could also be the emotional growth one experiences during a feat of that magnitude. In any event, five participants became four, and four became three. These final three managed to make it all within the 60-hour time limit. The first time the race had every experienced that number of finishers before. Making the total number of race victors to fourteen. Although I am unsure about the future years, and how many faired. I can assure you that the mentality behind the competition will more than likely remain the same, provided the same race officials are present, running the thing.

There are a few times in life when you experience true sportsmanship. Coming from a former athlete this means something. Human emotions, such as jealously, usually cloud the minds of some. This was the first time I had seen individuals be selfless. Everyone was selfless. It was less about a competition between racers, than a battle between you and yourself, for every runner present. The inability to complete all five rounds did not falter the desire of most expressing the will to return in years to come. Although they were hurting, exhausted, beaten down to the point of giving up, they lived for that challenge. That, as well as the unique qualities of the racecourse, is what made the experience oneofakind for so many people. The companionship built while out in the middle of nowhere is only understood by those who participated that year. They may not have been by each other's side together throughout the entire journey, but no matter the degree of success, they all shared in a life experience that is humbling even to the most experienced hiker, tracker, or physically active person. Especially for those who have made it through to the bitter end. That is what the Barkley Run inspires: humility.

For us all, in our current employment climate, there is excessive pressures to succeed. There are also other arenas that require you to succeed to the nth degree, as well. Like, for example, life. There are always certain milestones that occur within life that are usually expected at certain times. I have read numerous articles about women who prefer to have a career versus be a stay-at-home mom. I've even had these conversations within my own family and household. The reality of the situation is, when you decide to identify your success by other people's standards, or society's standards, you are falling short of what the purpose of life truly is. Life is about the journey. It doesn't matter who is able to accomplish what at the end of the day. We are all born, just as we all pass away. Yes, some with a higher monetary value can have more niceties and material objects at their disposal, but all too often you have to ask, are they really happy? Are they really enjoying life to the fullest potential? Are they even successful? We all want to rush around and do what has never been done before and make a name for ourselves and have pride doing that. But realistically, as long as you are devoting your time to what matters I am willing to argue wholeheartedly that you will wind up more successful in the long run. For those who love to work, which is the category I fall under, more power to you! I encourage you to make the best of your energy and time in that respect. However, I feel as though there is something more valuable in taking a minute to stop and smell the roses. Spain has taught me that there is nothing so important that you cannot wait. Having 2-3 hour meal times while in Spain has been an adjustment. But it has allowed me the opportunity to take a step back, enjoy and revel in the fact that I have this opportunity and I want to savor and live every minute of it.

If I am not successful at appreciating the positive aspects of my life, then maybe I do not deserve them. If I am not a person who cares for my friends and family enough to want to help them succeed, then maybe I do not deserve them either. One thing is for sure though, I will stop and take the time to measure the value of these things, and how successful I am at valuing them. No one can dictate that for me. No one can dictate whether or not I am capable and have reached my full potential. I have a friend of mine once tell me that I made a huge mistake by getting out of the Armed Forces, and I simply disagreed. Why, well because I wanted a career, but I also wanted the opportunity to have a family, to settle down, to parent any kids I may be blessed with. That could not happen if I were to be overseas fighting, nor could it happen if I were taken from this earth. I would never forgive myself if I didn't take the opportunity to be what I can be, in all aspects of what life has to offer.

Chapter 12

My Edu-mi-cation

Though the American culture values education and degrees, I have found that some of the most intelligent people have no degrees. I have been fortunate enough to afford not only a bachelor's degree, but also a master's. I feel as though they are both quite an accomplishment, especially considering I hate the structure of school, and most of the time I get grumpy over the subject matter. Yet I find myself learning more from individuals who are experienced in their line of work, or just have intelligence and not the means to attend schools like me. I think in this day and age it is practically impossible to get a job without a bachelor's degree, the exception being those who have been in the work force for years on end. Those who are more likely to find themselves employed have higher degrees, like a master's or PhD. With the job market being what it is, this should come as no surprise. People want only the best of the best working for them. They are searching for high energy, dedicated individuals who will work to the maximum level of efficiency in order to remain in the position. This is, of course, only pertinent to jobs that possess salary and potential benefits.

Minimum wage jobs are left to those who have not had the opportunities I have. Yet this may not be their fault. They may have been brought up in environments that do not provide the same kind of comforts that my middleclass upbringing brought for me. Forcing me to question whether or not our social system is truly set up in a way that marginalizes the same group of people, over and over again. Then we wonder why they resort to illegal means after trying to make legitimate jobs work. Frankly, minimum wage is not sufficient for anyone to live off of. Many individuals work multiple jobs just to break even, rendering the simple pleasures in life, like a vacation, impossible. Everyone deserves a break once in a while. Some individuals may squander their opportunities, this is true, yet others work harder than anyone in the upper echelon of society cares to admit.

For me personally, my education means very little. Sure, it looks great on paper, but this is one of the reasons I despise our current evaluating system. From the start, people are eliminated from the pool of vying applicants based upon credentials. Sure, some jobs require specific qualifications, but since when did we resort to eliminating people from the possibility of a future, based on things that may or may not have been their fault. They did not choose to grow up in the household, or with the financial standing that they had. Their parents' decision to procreate should not be a consequence left to punish future generations. Instead, if someone is taking the time to reach higher levels, and they can prove themselves capable, they should be given the opportunity to change their reality. Some of the most hardworking people I know have never been given that rare opportunity, the luck of someone taking a chance on them. Inspiring and motivating their potential, which leads me to wonder why that is. Why is it appropriate not to take a chance on people?

My educational background is so random that it makes me struggle to find the appropriate position. My undergraduate degree was a mixture between psychology, sociology and anthropology, and peace and global studies. I studied the human mind, its relationships to higher echelons, and how to mediate and navigate through generations of crisis. Since then, I have worked as a military police officer, and have had the opportunity to get certified by the FBI in basic negotiations. Yet I find myself still struggling to not only combine my experience and schoolwork to a formulated plan, to market myself for potential employment. Since I was sort of forced into a situation that reduced my chances for employment for three years, give or take, I made myself useful in other ways. I took on a position with the Department of the

Navy, helping others for more than two years, and I also worked towards furthering my education. While studying to get my Master's in Criminology, it occurred to me how different this was from Criminal Justice, and how that would hinder my ability to land a job in the future. While some of the same topics are covered, there are others that are not. With this sorted job and educational experience, where do I go from here? I cannot help but wonder what my options are. Do I go with a traditional job, or do I strive for a higher calling revolving around conflict resolution? If the latter is truly the direction I take my future, my master's degree is rendered almost obsolete. Extensively, I chose a path that serves my best desires in almost no way. Yet, I had no idea where I wanted to take my employment goals until recently. So, essentially, I may have just wasted time and energy, not to mention money and resources on a degree that may or may not be an applicable selling point.

This is just one of the many reasons I call my education, my edu-mi-cation. The certificate of completion, or diploma, says only that I managed to survive the time and course work required for the degree. It speaks in no way towards the difficulty or quality of the program. It also says nothing about how I did in the courses. Sure, I have transcripts, but truthfully, they do not tell the tale of my efforts, involvement, or capabilities. Only the professors I worked with truly know all that. Only the students I suffered alongside know that. I fully recognize that I could be just as capable or incapable as the next guy, regardless of what a piece of paper says. I value myself, my loyalty and dedication, but I do not place myself above others. I refuse to be condescending towards someone who has a different background, and I wish that the employment and education industries did the same.

I should mention that I am not downplaying the educational system or the weight of a degree necessarily, but I know people who cannot spell or formulate a sentence properly who earned degrees. How are these individuals somehow qualified to earn a degree? How are they better qualified than someone else without a degree? These are all things that one can only discern after employment has already begun. At which point, what is the benefit to the agency who hired them? They were willing to surpass other options, and for what? I guess my point is, you cannot judge a book by its cover. You cannot rely on paperwork to dictate whether or not someone is qualified. I do not believe the employment industry is set up to allow certain applicants a real chance at obtaining a position they are more than qualified for. This does not assist the work force in any way, shape, or form.

Personally, I rely on my wits, my ability to open my mind to new opportunities in order to dictate whom I choose to work with. I'm willing to go the extra mile and give someone an opportunity that once had little to no hope. My aim is to inspire those who believe they are somehow less of an individual, simply because of the circumstances of their youth that are completely unrelated to their abilities. Their contributions to society matter just as much as the next guy, and somehow, we have rendered them unimportant, immaterial, and incapable by traditional standards.

Chapter 13

Confusion and Utter Chaos

Growing up as someone who was adopted, and knew it from a very young age, there was a considerable amount of uncertainty in my life. As I look back, I now can recognize this was caused from a desire to have parents who had not been in the position to have their kids removed from their home, and eventually taken away on a more permanent basis. I spent many years trying to prove myself to my adoptive parents as I got older, and eventually it wore me down. The desire to avoid feeling guilt and shame was present, and I was always raised to be proud of my adoption, rather than ashamed of it. I always carried my head high and said it with pride, because I had overcome surmountable odds. Yet despite my largest attempts to do so, there was always something inside of me that made me feel like less of a person because of it, and in my weakest moments that would shine through.

As an infant I was taken into custody by the social services agency, given care and nursed back to health after suffering from malnutrition. My birth mother was given multiple opportunities to win her rights back but could never seem to get it together enough to do so. Appointments would be missed, unscheduled visits while intoxicated, and staying in an abusive relationship were all reasons as to why I eventually became a ward of the state. After spending some time in foster care, I was adopted by a couple who would later stay by my side through thick and thin, despite my efforts to alienate them.

Though I did not always get along with my adoptive parents, there were sometimes that were important. They afforded me the opportunity to be an athlete, learn piano, engage in languages and exploration of foreign countries, and more. That being said, there are some significant differences in opinion about the way things went down, in our house while growing up. That, however, is a different story, yet pertains to some complications of future events and emotions.

Feeling as though you have failed one set of parents, somehow, is a reality of many folks that have been adopted. Whether it be a baby girl from China who was disposed because of her gender, or an African child whose parents were killed during the civil unrest, there is always some sense of longing for a personal identity and connection with your past. Most have the stability of knowing where they came from, and the multitude of things that have led to their caliber of person in this day and age. I must say I got very lucky in that I did not end up in the foster care system, or worse, for the rest of my childhood. Especially considering I was older than two years old when I was adopted, which is considerably unusual. Normally, families are looking for little infants to raise from an earlier age, so those who remain in the system past that, or are taken into custody after their infancy are potentially seen as damaged goods. Who wouldn't want a teen that has experienced significant strife and uncertainty within the home? I mean really, that would incur additional effort on the part of the foster or adoptive parents, because by that point there is so much trauma built up that it is hard for anyone in that position to care. Especially considering they may be out on their own soon. But the same applies for children who are four, five, eight, or ten. They are way too old for families to be willing to take them in, and that reality is sad. Because those are the children that are rehabilitated. They can change with love, care, security, and attention. They can be molded into loving and dedicated contributors to society, provided they are secure in their attachment to a set of parents that will commit to them, despite their age. I have seen this time and time again, during my time working as a Youth Care Specialist for a residential youth care facility in Missouri.

The work there definitely provided me with my own brand of medicine. I healed in ways that I never thought possible, and for a time I sincerely believed that was my calling. I had always intended to get into that line of work, and somehow, I ended up there. It started out like any other job in this field, the kids testing your every move and decision. Until finally there was trust established. At that moment, you could see the climate of the cottage changing. When working with girls from eight to twenty-one, that's enough to drive anyone crazy. Add ten or fifteen of them in the same spot and you will want to tear your hair out on a good day! These kids were not broken, or damaged in any way. They were simply responding to how they had been treated in society. I initially worked in a cottage where most, if not all, of the kids were a ward of the state. They were there for a number of reasons, between parents having to get their stuff straight before having custody, to the kids acting out and requiring more extensive inpatient treatment. There was no telling how long each of these kids would stay, and they knew it. Some were committed to the system until they aged out. Most could handle this, some couldn't.

After a time, I switched to another cottage and worked with girls and boys, in the teenage bracket, who were more likely to stay shorter term. They were intelligent, focused, emotional beings that just needed guidance. There were adoption therapy groups, substance abuse prevention groups, anger management, and more specialized therapy sessions available to all the kids on the campus. These children knew, however, that they would soon be returning home. Some liked to think they knew how to play the system, while others gave up trying. A few even cared about their program and really wanted to get better, which was a rarity definitely worth spending time on.

I soon realized my time would have to end shortly, because after almost a year I was worn down. Having to see children float in day in and day out, with new attitudes and new crises, while the ones who showed improvement would leave made things quite exhausting. Another aspect was the physical component the job required in the event of crises. When you stick twenty girls together in the same cottage, all of whom are around the teen years, you are going to have crises, multiple crises per day. Depending upon the severity we would utilize holds with them and work towards processing through their emotions with them, until they were calm. Though it did not always go as ideal as that, most of the time you ended up with some degree of damage to your body by the end of the day. Whether it was a sixteen-hour shift, getting kicked, bitten, punched, or spat on, it was emotionally exhausting. Especially for someone who had already been there. I knew what it was like to hate to the degree these children did. I knew all too well what it was like to feel hopeless and depressed, because that was my reality. I was well aware that the only way I was to survive and ever dream of having kids of my own, was to get out. Move on. That was probably the most challenging thing to come to terms with, because we had been through some significant things together. Both the youth that I left, and the staff members.

The harsh reality of places like that are simple. Either they focus on keeping staff members, or they prefer to side with the kids. In the event that something did happen, I'm inclined to agree with the children, just in case. But when you have kids willing to make false allegations just to get someone they don't like in trouble, that ends the potential career in youth services for an individual. In many ways I felt stressed and unsure whether or not I would make it through another day, just because I feared that would happen to me. I valued the fact that this particular facility put the kids first. Don't get me wrong. Especially since other facilities in the area were known to be particularly harsh and almost downright abusive. Yet I couldn't help feel like it would only take one false accusation for them to can my ass.

Low and behold, I was accused of many things! I was called a bitch more times than I can count. I was told I was mean, and cruel. I was also accused of having vendettas against some of the children. All of which I saw as a cry for help. My experience told me that those comments were just excuses to justify wanting freedom, on the part of the child. They went from having little to no one caring for their welfare, to having rules and set guidelines, and as a result, they fought against it. This is the natural process of wild animals being tamed, is it not?

I was also accused of rape, when trying to put someone who was kicking me into a hold. Luckily there were other people within eyesight who knew exactly how far I was from the sort, which helped. After experiencing a multitude of riots and significant brawls, I left the place knowing that I would never return to that field of work. Not that I didn't want to help them but being hands on was in no way my favorite thing to do. Having to be hated on daily was not my favorite part of the job either. In fact, I still have a scar on my shoulder where I was bitten nearly four years ago. Although this was the one time someone was in a genuine state of crisis, versus vying for attention, it hurt like hell, and I have a permanent reminder of the experience!

Like any ride or die position, like the military, you bond with your colleagues in a way that is rare. I still talk to my old friends and coworkers from that place, because we went through a substantial amount together, having each other's back the entire time. We would face up to children who would become the equivalent of the hulk, completely aware we might get punched in the face or worse, and yet all parties came out relatively unscathed. We would lighten the mood by cracking jokes and playing pranks on each other, to keep things particularly interesting. Some of the jokes we shared with the residents, but most were kept private, between us, so that we could have inside jokes to laugh about when things got really rough.

Although social services employment is a challenge, day in day out without a question, there are some aspects of being in an environment like that which give you a particular awareness of how close to the prison system some of these kids are. After seeing a number of children float in and out multiple times, before finally leaving the last time, there isn't a day that goes by where we don't remember and reflect on the actions of one or two of our "favorite" residents. Some of the residents have wound up in newspaper issues about some offense that has winded them up in jail or prison. Some have aged out of the system, so they have no other place to go but jail. Others have wound up in mental institutions for their failure to work their individualized programs.

To say all of these experiences have brought clarity and insight into my own life would not be sufficient in describing how I feel. There are moments that bring back my experiences (vivid memories), which usually result in an elevated heart rate, sweat, heavy breathing, alertness, etc. There is nothing that can undo what I feel about my circumstances. I must come to terms with that. So many kids wind up in situations like this. It is the lucky few who have the ability to come out on top that makes me wonder even more so, why me? Why is it that my struggle is so much so that it haunts me, yet has allowed me motivation to succeed in life? As I continue to push forward, to aim to change myself for the better by reducing aggression, violence, hate and anger, it is only natural that I feel like somehow, I don't deserve the lifestyle I have been given. The opportunities to succeed that have presented themselves. The ability to look disaster in the eye and not let it define who I am. This relates to the importance of music I mention, where it fuels the soul, and depending upon the music one prefers to listen to, they can be swayed one way or another. Although there were times I listened to very hateful music, and occasionally still do, I know it does not define who I am as a person. That is apparent in my day-to-day actions.

I am defined only by what my closest peers think. How I treat them, whether I support them in dire circumstances, and how I demonstrate respect for their individuality are all factors. The latter is a lost art, in many ways. It is my personal belief that discussing viewpoints is what makes us more intelligent, and open minded. Some may understand how circumstances beyond your control have shaped you, while others may not. It does not diminish a person's worth to not understand, but how they treat you following that moment may define whether they are valuable to you. Kindness goes a lot farther than any alternative. Empathy does just the same. We all have different backgrounds. We all have been scared at some point. Scarred even. It is how we approach the resolution of each of these situations that expresses us as human beings.

Chapter 14

The Zombie Apocalypse

I don't know how many folks entertain a convoluted notion, or know someone that does, but my husband did me dirty. He waited until after I said "I do", to tell me that the zombie apocalypse was real. His plan (yes, he has a plan) has been in the works for years. He has been waiting for that down ass bitch to contribute somehow to the survival of the fittest. I shit you not. I am way in over my head with this one. I don't even know where to begin. First off, since I was in the Army and my husband can only navigate the seas, I am to get us to the coast. From there, my husband will take over and sail us to Louisiana, because that is where he is from, wants to retire to, and has friends worth saving. From arrival to the United States, I will once again lead the way to get to the communicated rendezvous location, between a group of boys, now grown into men. Think I'm done yet? Ha! Nope! This goes on! From there, we will gather additional resources and weapons that we don't already possess, and that we have not already acquired. I may have prefaced this with the fact that we have more than enough guns, so many knives and daggers I can't count them all, axes of all shapes and sizes (with various purposes too, I might add), one set of brass knuckles, and one brass knuckle taser. (Guess who that's for!) Oh, and a wooden samurai training sword just in case shit gets categorically fucked. So, I think the weapons we might be good on, because that's just the stash my husband and I maintain after three and a half years of marriage. And the other dudes are even more batshit crazy than we are. I say that in a loving way, of course. So, upon meeting we will find a holding point and fight to survive by acquiring additional food and potentially starting our own farm. Ironically, I grew up with a garden, as did my husband, so we get to take turns planting and harvesting edibles.

I think the most shockingly devastating point to this story is these individuals' worth saving. As much as I love them, it's utterly amazing that these two have half a brain. Yet, they are ridiculously intelligent. Both having engineer experience. My concern lies in the fact that these are the individuals who convinced my husband to eat half a notebook during his younger days. Literally, eat half a notebook. So, as for how we will manage to survive I don't know. Because if shit hits the fan, I promise you, I won't be eating paper for survival. I will be killing anything that moves and comes within ten feet of me that I don't immediately recognize. If you are lucky to get close enough to me to be within striking distance, know that I have an unhealthy fascination with knives, daggers, and tasers. No bullshit. Oh, and 50 Cal machine guns, I LOVE them. God help the soul who pisses me off pre-apocalypse. Never mind post-apocalypse. Just saying.

Chapter 15

Facing Demons

For anyone with time served in a military branch, they have given their lives in support of a higher purpose, which is American freedom. Whether you are liberal or conservative, whether you believe in violence and military action or not, it is safe to say that in certain circumstances, the military is a necessary tool. I have never been ignorant to this fact, but it wasn't long ago that I was a dirty hippy, a term I giggle about when used. I went to a Quaker school that had very few conservatives in its population. Yet war was something I understood as a necessity. While I did not always agree with the implementation of the military, I knew to possess it was the only way any country could stay safe in this day and age.

The controversy surrounding our former and current presidents, or how they used the Constitution or failed it, is effectively irrelevant. None of that matters when you are inside a branch of service. What matters, is that that is your Commander in Chief. What he or she says, goes. Some may believe that Clinton was a better option, but in my personal opinion, I doubt that very much. Although some claim her to be a strong role model for women everywhere, I believe there are people who are better applicants for that position. Simply put, from a military standpoint, we are bred to make a decision when leaders, and stick to it. Clinton has shown her inability to do so. Another thing bred into us, is loyalty, selfless service, and accountability for our actions through the Uniformed Code of Military Justice, which holds strict guidelines for all military personnel. While I agree that not every member is above reproach, I can say without a doubt that had Clinton been accountable, she would have admitted her wrongdoing, and faced the consequences of her actions or inactions.

This is all said while maintaining full awareness that I do not know her personally, and there is much debate about whether or not the media paints an accurate position. Regardless, those are significant issues when dealing with war, terrorism, and the lives of so many people who have devoted their lives to protecting our country. Though there are many more who have applied and been refused, these individuals have agreed to salaries that are in many ways, insufficient. They have families who endure the sacrifice with them, by experiencing deployments, hectic lifestyles, working their own jobs, and rearing children alone. To say this is a family commitment is not enough. Many marriages do not make it through the copious challenges the military requires of its members. The percentage of divorce and extramarital affairs within the confines of the military is astounding. With all of life's challenges that can confront a marriage, given enough time, respect should be afforded to the families of military service members, just as much as the warriors. After all, they sacrifice what many take for granted, in order to provide safety and security for individual opinion, no matter how biased it may be. Judgement does not fall on the heads and hearts of military members. As obvious as that sounds, I feel it is necessary to say as much. Yet, judgement should be waged in the wake of the civil unrest occurring with a nation so many serve to protect.

My time serving as an Army officer was unique, to say the least. There is nothing traditional about being thrown into a leadership position at the age of twenty-four, yet I like to believe I stepped up to the task. I was one of the fortunate ones who had completed college and spent time out in the work force before joining. It was for my own personal reasons and the desire to find self-worth that I agreed to sign up. Yet, there was also a desire to work amongst people who valued each other. To build lifelong friends, which I soon discovered was a definite possibility. Despite taking considerable time for training, I soon found myself with an amazing support system within the military, and I was off to my first duty station, Guantanamo Bay, Cuba (GTMO).

For most, this would be a daunting first assignment, and I would lie if I didn't admit there was some degree of insecurity and doubt about the purpose of this facility. Once arriving and having access to the inside, so to speak, I soon found myself relieved at the humanity that maintained, despite accusations to the contrary. As I prepared myself for the grueling year ahead, filled with night shifts and day shifts, multiple rotations within a mere week between both shifts, and being responsible for multiple Soldiers, I was excited. Motivated, even, by the tasks ahead. To say there were moments if I wondered if I would be successful, is an understatement. There were moments when I realized I would either have to suck it up or fail. Luckily, I have never quite accepted failure as part of my life. I do not like being told no, just as I do not like failing others.

My main priority as a leader, became gaining the respect of the people I was responsible for, and remaining neutral to the multitude of conflicts that I was to be faced with. Because sure as I'm a woman, working in a man's world during this period, there were conflicts a plenty. Once the initial shock wore off, things started to fall into place. I realized the importance of my position, my desire to protect my subordinates from the unnecessary, and a desire to have the best intentions with regards to interacting with detainees, despite what they may think. At one point, I was told it was not me personally they hated, but the uniform. I had a very different rapport with every detainee. Some tried to manipulate me over time, while others just gave up hope that they could bend or sway my judgement. Other individuals that worked in the facility may or may not have liked me, but my desire to be liked was unimportant and irrelevant in that role. I was there to do a job, as difficult as it may be, and I was there to protect and serve my people, just as much as we were all there to protect and serve our country.

There isn't a day that goes by that I don't reminisce about the things I learned about myself and others within that facility. I learned to trust my team, through experience, even though a certain degree of trust was placed in them initially. Though there were always some that were the odd men or women out, there were more that were amazing at what they did, despite having moments of doubt or uncertainty as to why. My job was to ease that conflict within them, and to motivate them to continue to do their job with their heads held high. One thing that frequently goes unnoticed is the intent to harm, on the part of detainees. They don't care that they have diseases when they throw feces, urine, or blood your way. In fact, most of them are painfully aware that they possess such and are more than willing to threaten the lives of others with bodily fluids, in order to attack their perceived enemy in any way possible. Nor do they care if they harm another person, because they have committed their life to a cause that seemingly all but died the moment they entered our facilities more than a decade or two ago.

There are many issues with confinement. Anyone who works in a facility will tell you that. But after being inspired to complete my master's thesis equivalent on the history of terrorism, particularly within ISIS, I can honestly say that this was a whole new brand of crazy. Religious quotes being contorted by zealots who see themselves as saviors for people, but whom also have hidden agendas that involve gaining political influence and power. The destruction of others is necessary to build strength. Strength is required by resources, followers, and as much damage that can be caused is necessary to be achieved as such. The more educated, the more valuable. Recruiters, teachers, students, and sacrificial lambs all aid in the successful completion of the tasks various leaders initiate. The particular difference between ISIS and other groups like al-Qaida being their willingness to kill other Muslims, which I believe I have already discussed. In the world of confinement, the lifelong dedication of any terrorist network, however, makes lengthy detainment irrelevant. They maintain the desire to sacrifice themselves, if necessary, to put a negative light on the infidels.

Within GTMO this was no different. So, as if regular confinement operations are not already difficult enough, you now have an international element added into the mix. Especially since there is the misconception that all confinement practices are the same. The truth is, they are not. GTMO was, and probably still is, run on a different set of rules. The people confined there are detainees. While there may be some individuals convicted within a tribunal and are treated along the lines of traditional confinement operations. Most would be considered international detainees. Confined because of various behaviors that have led authorities to believe they have taught, recruited, learned from, and participated in a movement whose primary purpose is to cause fear in the international community. Make no mistake, these people are not innocent. They were not rounded up for the first time and shipped off to a faraway place. These were repeat offenders, at the very least. Yet still, they possess certain rights that are not afforded by traditional confinement procedures.

No matter the agenda of the international community, it was never and is never a guard force member's authority to treat them any different than any other prisoner or detainee. For all intents in purposes, since previous negative images and circumstances came to light, GTMO was reformed by way of procedure. Despite the accusations of released detainees, treatment was humane. Procedures were put in place for their security, even when they intended to harm themselves or others. There were a multitude of challenging moments, to say the least, and each one seemed new and different than the last. With the change of staff ever revolving at one duty assignment or another, there is no doubt that after being confined for over ten or so years, every detainee knew protocol better than the guard force. We trained and trained and confronted every situation with the same rigor and guidelines afforded to us, but I can honestly tell you, there is nothing like staring an evil man dead in the face. He may not be evil because of what he has been rumored to have done. He is evil in his actions towards you individually, while simultaneously claiming his actions are a universal attack, and not personal. That ordinarily, he has come to like you, yet the circumstances warrant him to put that aside.

Mental warfare is in no shortage at this facility, and any others located in theater (overseas). That may very well be an understatement. Yet surprisingly, like most, I survived my time there, and grew, as a direct result of my involvement. I also watched many others find themselves in various ways, whether it was a death in the family they were not home for, the demise of a relationship with a loved one, a run-in with a career ending health concern, or more. For me personally, I grew patience. Something I knew very little about when I first undertook the assignment. I had always understood myself to be every bit the Taurus I am. Bullheaded, if you will, which meant that I was stubborn, impulsive, and not at all patient. Simultaneously, I could demonstrate understanding, concern, caring for my job and for my subordinates, and a desire to see everyone succeed in their respective positions. Getting promoted, coming out a better person in a better position, is what I soon wanted for everyone. The hardest thing I have ever had to challenge myself with, was letting go when the time was right. Despite having had a wonderful time, like most things, they come to an end. That end was heart wrenching. I had lost friends who had arrived before me, and gained new ones, and now it was my time to leave. Despite my physical departure, a part of me will always remain there, not because I loved the lifestyle. I actually hated it in some ways, namely the unrelated challenges I faced on the outside of the camp walls. The part I miss was the comradery, the trust built through repeated decisions on everyone's part, to make the right call and stick with it. To be able to assist any and every-one when they were in need. To be able to know that if something bad happened to anyone present, there was an accountability that would take place within our ranks, or from higher. While there were plenty of tough times, this is what made it all worthwhile. The system, and the people within. The knowledge that for every action there is a consequence, or a greater or equal reaction. It may not always appear to exist all the time, but the majority of the time, that is what held us all together. The ability to know one another inside and out and be able to stand next to any individual and know that you would pull through the toughest of nights not for yourself, but for them. Because crisis never happens when you're prepared for it, it always happens when you're feeling weak, drained, or at your worst. Though every day possessed some sort of crises, the men and women who I was lucky enough to meet made me get up each morning, and face the day, even when I felt I had nothing left to give.

Chapter 16

Knives, Tasers, & Weapon Systems

During my time in the Army, I grew to appreciate various weapons and useful self-defense techniques to their fullest! I have an unhealthy fascination with knives, and I get quite excitable when I see a taser in action. In fact, the more the merrier! To make matters potentially worse, I have really grown to appreciate military grade weapon systems. After carrying a 240B or 249B around with me while traipsing through the woods to complete training, anyone would either love or hate those machine guns. Nevertheless, my heart utterly melts with the 50cal. I was lucky enough to be assigned to that weapon system for numerous weeks and loved being in a turret and pressing the butterfly trigger! It sends all sorts of vibrations down your spine, which is a feeling only imaginable to most.

My house is chalked full of most of these crazy items. From daggers to hand-held knives, to k-bars who could not be in heaven, realistically!? My husband's fascination with all things Viking and potentially medieval has landed us a considerable number of throwing axes, a double-sided axe we purchased in Germany during a trip over the holidays, and a tomahawk style axe for fun. My husband even set up his own throwing axe station in the back yard and has on multiple occasions barely missed our oblivious dog, Fallon. To make matters worse, there is a fancy brass knuckle taser that was gifted to me for some special occasion I can no longer remember. Even though it is not really brass and more like plastic, it emits an amazing zap! If anyone has had the pleasure of getting one of those electronic buzz zappers, it sounds like that! The directions for such a beast of a contraption are downright hilarious! Like most sets of directions, it begins quite mundanely, but it quickly gets to the good part! The part where it tells you step by step how the gradual increase in contact time against an individual can result in various levels of discombobulation! For half a second, discomfort and potential confusion. For a full second, pain and irritation. A second and a half results in significant pain and potential weakness in the knees. After two seconds, weakness in the knees, substantial pain and the possibility of falling. After three seconds, well, a person just loses it! Falling is guaranteed, the obvious yelp and mental disassociation. In what world is this item something you can buy willynilly!? It results in disassociation! I love it!

I guess something must be said for my extreme irritation in movies these days, where hand systems (45s, 9mm, etc.) can be used to shoot people over 100 feet away. At this point, realistically, you are bound to hit something that you don't intend to hit. Let's be honest, research is quite easy to accomplish now that the internet has everything you could want to find, and then some. It pays to do a little research before getting into a situation that will only waste ammunition, and not benefit anyone. In fact, you do more harm than good, even if it is just a stunt. Let's not get me started on the range of a M2 50 cal. It is well over 6,000 meters. This machine is meant to fire obstacles from miles away. Using it within a 25-meter range is absurd. To anyone who knows better, it ruins a decent action flick. I recently watched a movie where someone utilized the equivalent of an AT4 rocket launcher within a few feet of themselves. This would result in your demise. Literally, you're dead. Exploded into tiny bits and pieces, and the world would laugh at your stupidity. The kind of dark humor that you find when you watch videos of terrorists trying to figure out how to work weapon systems, and either end up blowing themselves and their comrades into eternity, or they end up on their ass because they did not support themselves properly, and the weapon system goes off a cliff. Safety first people, safety first. I understand you're just trying to make a movie, but there is a certain degree of ignorance in the general population which begs to be called out.

I will admit that for a time I was ignorant about the military and all it offers you. For those who have loved ones in any branch of service, the amount of training they undergo is substantial. Is there a threat to their safety? Yes. It is inherent with their job description. Yet, they are trained. One must recognize that they are also the most feared entity within the world, as far as military operations go. We have maximized the ability to perform uniformly, and within the confines of researched tactics. Even while training other forces to do a simple task, they are known to flea out of fear. Our military does not, because we have the desire to protect our friends to the left or right of us. Maybe not ourselves so much, but most definitely our battle buddies. You will hear stories of people selflessly sacrificing themselves by using their body as a shield for grenades and such, and the math is simple. Do I sacrifice the lives of everyone in the area, or just myself? One mourning family is better than five, six, or even ten. While there are parameters which usually make that many casualties in one area, there are also circumstances that cannot be helped.

Another thing to consider is that many of the folks that join the service have families of their own. Wives, kids, parents, and other friends and family members that are worth protecting. The requirement of selfless service is written very plainly as a promoted mindset to have, once entering the service. You will never find closer friends than those who have experienced some degree of battle together. There are still people I keep in touch with whom I have not seen since 2009. That's an outstanding eight years, yet we are thick as thieves. I once had a Soldier of mine be insulted by someone who was of equal rank to me. I quickly stepped in and took over the situation, and before I knew it, I had lost a "friend" because of my inability to choose their side over my former soldiers'. That is not a friend worth keeping, in my opinion. The respect of your people is only earned by being able to understand their position, support them in everything they do, and guard them from the insanities present in all institutions. That was my goal, and I like to think it paid off.

Most importantly, it is not the weapon systems that keep you safe, regardless of training. Although they are enthralling in and of themselves, it is the person to your left and right that make it worthwhile to continue to play with things that kill people. That may sound slightly ridiculous, but without them, there would be no point. Yes, we are all repeatedly attacked with safety tips during training, but the reality of your circumstances only becomes real when you are standing next to someone you have grown to know and love, while having a life-threatening scenario in front of you.

Chapter 17

Bienvenidos a Espana!

If you ever have the opportunity to travel around Europe, do it. I have been lucky enough to live here for almost three full years. Although I have lived in foreign countries before, Europe is an entirely different experience because of the proximity of each and every nation that it encompasses. Although Spain is one of the most interesting and historical countries there are, in my opinion, beauty and history can be found throughout this region of the world. I have learned interesting facts while here. Spain was the country that founded Christopher Columbus and has a fairly short distance between it and Africa. In fact, there is a town a few hours from here that is on the southern-most tip of the country and offers ferry rides back and forth. It is that distance that has made it susceptible to Arabic rule over the years, and so you can discover a wide variety of influences both from Arabic and Christian heritage.

There are a substantial number of must-see cities in this country as well. Up north there's Barcelona, in the middle of the country lies the capital, Madrid. Farther down south you have Seville, a fantastic place to visit during Semana Santa (holy week), and on the southeast coat lies a huge resort town known as Malaga. Other cities, like Valencia (home of paella), Ronda (a city included in the "white villages" group, and also the home of bullfighting), and of course Rota and El Puerto de Santa Maria (Puerto). In the Andalusian region, the southernmost region, you will also have the opportunity to visit the region's capital, Cadiz, which has a huge Mardi Gras equivalent festival each year. Or Jerez de la Frontera, which is home to local bodegas who specialize in sherry wine, fresh meats from their ranches, and tons of assorted olives. Not that any other location in Spain is short on the supply of these three things, but it is a closer option for us in particular. Rota and Puerto have their respective charms, and beaches galore. In fact, the population here swells three times its original population during the summer months. Tourists from all over Europe come down and spend their summers here, just for the beach experience! Ironically, that is also the best time to vacate this area and explore other locations in Europe.

Every year Semana Santa (holy week) occurs throughout the country. Floats donning real silver and gold, depicting the religious events surrounding Easter, are hand-carried down the streets of every town. To participate in these processions is an honor. To carry a float is one of the highest honors. After practicing for months on end, carrying the weight on the backside of your neck while maintaining the beat of every step, you feel accomplished in a sense that it is a sacrifice for what Jesus experienced during this short week. It is about self-sacrifice and personal growth on a spiritual level, to endure everything that goes into this process.

Following this experience by a few short weeks comes Feria, the spring festival. Jerez de la Frontera is usually the city that begins the season of the Spring Festivals. This will go on for a few days in each city, and there will be a rotation of events in every town in Spain. The final Feria usually occurs in Ronda, during the beginning of September. So, you can imagine the degree of energy put into preparing for this season as well. Locals will purchase three or four Flamenco dresses and rotate them each year, depending upon location, until they have worn all of them to the different towns. They will go to ferreterias (hardware stores) and trade out their dresses for new ones, which they will wear the next few years. No joke! Dancing, drinking, food, and rides are all a specialty during these festivals. Every town prides themselves for their accomplishments. Horse and carriage rides are available, as are horse shows and bullfights. It is a wonderful experience to have, and only some Americans will take the time to buy a dress and go to Feria wearing the full accessorized attire. Even fewer will take the time to learn the dance and have the courage to go into a booth and partake in the dance party. Every booth (and there are many) hosts a different purpose. Some have food, others are bars, some restaurants, and even more are organized by different groups within the community, who usually have an open area for dancing. You will see disco club dancing and cultural dancing.

There are bodegas all around to visit and tour, and even more opportunities for ethnic food. Since bulls and cows are a plenty in this area, there is meat from various regions which is spectacular. In this particular area near Rota and Puerto, the land is fertile and is used for farming. Vegetables and fruits are grown without pesticides and herbicides, and it is obvious. It is a traditional daily habit for locals to walk to the shops and gather the products they will use during that day to make a meal. Since the food is all natural, it lasts a shorter period of time. However inconvenient this may sound to the odd American, it is an opportunity to engage in social interaction.

Spanish culture is deeply immersed within the family unit. Spain overcame a dictatorship in 1975, so the entire country is extremely poor. You will find families of three or four generations living together in the same household. Children live with their parents even after they are married, in some situations. Schooling is a privilege and is considerably more challenging than the American school system. While they are taught an extensive amount, their salaries are not comparable to anything you will find elsewhere. Doctors and surgeons in the United States make excessive amounts, yet in Spain they barely make anything, for example. That is the reality here. No one really seems to mind though. The basis for their lives is enjoying every minute they can. Workdays start at ten in the morning, and at one-thirty or two in the afternoon they take siestas, which warrants them approximately three hours to spend eating with the family and taking short naps before progressing with their day. Later in the evening people will return to work and continue on to about nine or ten at night. They will go home, eat dinner, and prepare for their nightlife which can sometimes span into the wee hours of the morning. They will get up the next day and repeat the cycle.

The inherent social nature is part of the reason criminality is limited. For minor offenses, the family is left to rehabilitate their odd man or woman out, and they will usually suffer a fine. Serious offenses will be punished with jail time, however the sheer numbers of people imprisoned is significantly small in comparison to that of the United States. An interesting side note to their social standard is that publicly offending a woman will automatically guarantee you jail time. Even as a foreigner. If you are seen to be accosting a woman, be it verbally or physically, you will pay dearly. Yet another thing absent in American culture. The role of the woman, the mother, the sister, the grandmother is a respected position. They are the ones who will continue the family line, and while they are generally perceived as strong and potentially fierce characters, they will be respected at all costs.

— *Chapter 17.25* —

International Travel from Espana

During my time in this amazing country, I have had the opportunity to go on a cruise, visit Germany, and travel throughout Italy. My cruise encompassed a seven-day excursion to multiple locations within France and Italy, Montenegro, and Greece. Although we were only given a day to travel around each town (or in many cases two towns), the experience was not lost on me. Most of these locations have some hop-on, hop-off tour bus, which takes you around to all the important sights. For the cities without this option, finding that hole in the wall eatery and small community to spend most of your time is preferable. It is amazing what you can pick up just by watching people. Each and every city has their own specialty, be it leather products, limoncello, award-winning chocolate, and more. Every time you turn around you are witnessing an entirely unique variation of a culture you never thought could be so diverse.

My husband and I went to Germany over Thanksgiving one year. Although we went to an Army resort in the southern part of the country, we spent most of our time outside of the base experiencing tours of the various attributes the area had to offer. From monasteries that produced their own brand of beer, cheese and wooden products, to castles, natural hikes, and brewery tours. Although we spent a considerable amount of money making our days filled with entertainment, there were also a few lazy days planned as well. We got to experience drinks in a pub that was formerly the headquarters of the SS. We ate a typical German meal while watching some boys dance authentically to traditional music. And need I mention the Christmas markets we were lucky enough to experience that early in the season. Though Garmisch and Partenkirchen are neighboring towns they historically despise one another. We were lucky enough to see the competition between the towns depicted in their gatherings and Christmas market booths. They had music, dance, and the entire community came out to celebrate their respective festivals.

Chapter 17.75

Italia

My next trip worth boasting about was to Italy. Although I had seen many of the cities a friend and I went to during this trip, I was able to experience more than just a few hours walking around. This led to a better understanding of their lifestyle, food, music, and historical sights. We went to Rome, Florence, Pisa, and eventually ended in Venice. Venice stole my heart! Since I was a young child and a piano player, I always wanted to experience this city first-hand after listening to my Vivaldi's Four Seasons tape as a kid. It provided me with an escape of sorts. My mind would wander to the canals, the food, the potential for a far-away land. It ended up being every bit I hoped it would be, and then some. We spent New Year's living the life Venice style, got to meet up with the husbands who had been gone for a bit, and learn what exactly made this part of Italy so unique. Stores with handmade masks ended up being our financial downfall (and we left with way too many), the various high-end shops, the religious relics, and a small pub that reminded me of the place I met my husband. Although it was difficult trying to get from one place to another with luggage, due to the multitude of little bridges, it was well worth the time spent.

I spent multiple days in Rome, Florence, and got to see the Leaning Tower of Pisa. Although the Tower was a fifteenminute experience it was interesting to see an iconic building that I had heard so much about as a kid.

It was interesting to hear the historical rivalry between Florence and Rome and their battle over who which be the capital of Italy. Over the course of time that honor has been rotated between the two cities, but the pride evident by the tour guides demonstrated just how much glory was affiliated with obtaining that title.

The culture did not stop there. The copious amounts of leather shops and restaurants were to die for. Leatherwork was somewhat of a talentand that I was completely unaware of prior to my journey. The wine was fantastic, as was the Prosciutto that melts in your mouth, available at every restaurant and in bulk at supermarkets. (A tradition shared by more than just this country.)

Something I did not expect was the Duomos, or churches, in nearly every city. I should have known, given how prevalent Catholicism is in that region, but they pride themselves in these massive architectural masterpieces. It made me wonder what I was in comparison. There were cobblestone pathways, public art and statues that are world renown. And the infamous Italian gelato. Yet another food that simply melts in your mouth. Not too sweet, but just sweet enough to beg you to return for more!

The experiences I cultivated from my time travelling has been one of the main highlights of my entire life. The history I have managed to witness that far outdates anything the United States has to offer truly enlightened me. I am in awe with how many historical conflicts we Americans have only read about in books, but in Italy and other European countries it is extraordinarily evident just in a religious sense alone. Mosques, temples, and churches are a must-see in nearly every location you go when doing the standard tourist activities in countries like that. The public evidence of the history that is present within another part of the world truly had me inspired and is something I encourage everyone to try and witness at least once in their life.

Chapter 18

Unadulterated Anger

One night I was out with the husband and some friends, just having a great time. Anyone who knows me understands that I have a fascination with playing pool and understanding the dynamics of the game to the maximum potential. While I will never, or more than likely never, make it to the professional level, I have been known to be a bit of a shark in my time. Despite not playing for a few years, and being terribly inconsistent, I opted to play that night at a local bar. I was minding my own business following a win, when a guy came up, put his money in and began racking the balls. Nothing new. His acquaintance came up to me and asked me if I was any good. I told him I haven't played in a while, but I'm decent. He continued on to say that his friend was egotistical and needed a lesson that would knock him down a few pegs. I told him I would do what I could. We talked for a few moments and exchanged names, and to my surprise I recognized the name. I asked him whether or not he was affiliated with my husband's command, and to my surprise I was responded to with an accusation of trying to pull rank. For anyone not affiliated with the military, this means that he was accusing me of trying to make myself out to be better than him. Which was not my intent. I knew his name from somewhere and took a stab in the dark to discover whether or not this was someone my friends out with me would know.

After he finished with his hostile comments, I simply explained that that was not my intent. That I was a civilian and had no rank. But that I worked in a position, recognized the name and thought maybe he was affiliated with some of the people I knew. Before I knew what happened, I was accused of being racist because all South Americans must be the same, right? Yet again I was put on the defensive and more than insulted about being seen as racist. I have never judged anyone by the way they look, despite my upbringing in American culture which seems to want to dictate that impression for everyone. Yet I kept my cool and explained that when I was out of the house and floating around town, this was the environment I usually would meet people I hadn't met before. I continued on to explain that I meant no offense, and I was certainly one to avoid judging people by their skin color, orientation, religion, or origins. I then explained who my husband was, and why I thought maybe they knew each other, and before I could get more than a word or two in, he started explaining his position of authority to me, and how the military ranking system works.

Although I was willing to hear him out, I did everything I could to immediately exit the situation, because no matter how much I tried, it was clear this guy was not going to see me in any less offensive manner. I went over to my husband who had been watching the entire dynamic evolve and explained briefly what had happened. He wasn't a fan, because as I've probably explained before now, he's very protective. So, I continued on and began to play my game of pool, with the full intention of not giving the acquaintance what he had asked an ass kicking for his friend. So, as I putzed around the table for a bit, and let the other guy come out on top, other friends who had noticed the conflict and overheard some of it, came over to inquire about it. I simply explained that the guy was aggressive and that was that. They expressed their intent to have my back, in the event such was necessary, and they quickly went back to their night, elsewhere and close by. If there's one thing about the military, you have brothers and sisters in arms, and although I was no longer in a military branch, I had earned the respect of those around me. Enough to make them comfortable doing whatever was necessary. Before the close of the game, I approached the aggressor one last time, and explained to him that I harbored no ill will, and if and when I would see him around base, bygones would be bygones. Yet again I was met with a look of disgust at such a suggestion. That he might find himself in a position to interact with me ever again. I explained that the base was small, and that given my husband's similar rank, that I was almost certain we would find ourselves face to face one more. After an utterly confused look came over the guy's face, he asked me to explain what I meant. I reminded him that I had mentioned that maybe they knew each other in our previous conversation, because they were of similar standing. He claimed to have not heard that at all, and I believed him. From that point on, his demeanor towards me changed completely. He approached my husband and tried to befriend him and went so far as to buy my friends and I shots. I thanked him but reiterated that there was no ill will.

This was a clear and decisive moment for me in time. Despite being continuously antagonized for who knows what reason, I managed to rise above my initial instinct to be aggressive. I knew that meeting anger with anger hardly ever solves a situation well. Therefore, having the inner courage to suck it up and take it, would later pay off. As far as I can tell, it did. There is something to be said for leaving a conversation making another person feel like the asshole they may or may not have been. That happens to be a strong suit of mine, through years of learning exactly what buttons to push, and how to push them. Language is a very powerful thing. The words used in a conversation can usually be crafted to your advantage, if you have the will to do so. There is never a moment in time where I doubted that this guy was going to leave that night feeling every ounce of confusion he left me with. Was that wrong, possibly. But I stood up for myself in a way most people don't have the courage to do. I made sure I did not internalize the accusations made, and I simply suggested in a less than obvious manner that assuming things about someone you don't know, whom you approached, is probably not a good idea. The seed had been planted, and before long I was on my way home.

This being said, I understand all too well what it means to be angry. For years I was scarred by my own actions. I was angry, I hated everything, and I had no remorse for my actions. I literally woke up one day and realized that I did not like the person I was becoming, and before long I started to teach myself, day in and day out, how to withhold the urge to pounce whenever I was antagonized. This is easier said than done. My tongue was my nemesis for quite some time! I realized exactly how difficult it was to say that I wanted to change, but actually face the ability to stop and not complete an initial, knee-jerk reaction. My hatred was the cause of a lot of anger. For a while I could not fathom why it was that I was alive. I could not understand why I had survived, been given some opportunities and not others, and was unable to piece together the reasons for putting me through all the pain and strife I experienced. Why not just end my life back when I could not care for myself? To me, my concentrations on what did not seem to make sense were my largest enemy. Little did I know I was to spend years contemplating questions I still don't know the answers to. There are some things about which I will never know the "why". While part of me is unsettled because of that, other parts are just flat out relieved. I am relieved that I can let go of this ideal that I must have the answer to everything. Although I do not do well when I don't get my way, and I'm incredibly stubborn, for once my mind is at peace with the knowledge that the answers I sought don't matter.

Over the years I have realized that the why's and the how's matter not. The two things in life that are guaranteed are being born and dying. These are inevitable. There is little one can do to avoid these. The decision to have a child is not the child's own, and it took me years to become okay with this. I hated that I was never consulted on my being born. Life did not make sense to me. But sure as you are born, it is inevitable that one must die. That's the nature of all living things. When one goes, however, people do not stop and consider the what if's of that person's life. The person is clearly incapable of contemplating what could have happened, if... Therefore, why do we spend so much time trying to figure out what could have been, if this is in no way pertinent to our ultimate demise? We spend so much time worrying about the material things, the here and now, and the monetary value of our contributions to society, yet what do we have to show for it? It isn't like we take our riches to our grave, or our job titles or socioeconomic positions. So again, I ask why is it that in today's society, we focus on these ridiculous notions?

Those who believe in religion frequently are concerned in the type of being they are. They go to church on Sunday, every week, and they pray and genuflect, and they ask for forgiveness. Some may even confess their sins. Yet I have very seldom met a person who attends services that walks out of that church following the sermon to continue the life lessons preached in that day's sermon. Every week they are confessing the same sins, time and time again, expecting a different result. I get that we are only human, but at what point are you acting a role instead of internalizing an intent to honestly change yourself? My conclusion to all this, after some significant thought, is that religion matters not. Spirituality matters. Your faith matters, in a higher power, or in the ability for you to change for the better. For you to contribute to the community in a way that is deserving of warranting a spot in "heaven", or whichever eternal place you believe in. It is the caliber of character that I seek out. Life will always be a purpose for the betterment of humankind. I can get mad, make mistakes, and genuinely have rough or less than stellar moments. But to find a balance, to stop asking why, to avoid getting drawn into the materialistic rigmarole, and to stop and actually smell the roses and enjoy the journey of a lifetime. That is my goal. Before I know it, my life will come to an end. It may be tomorrow, a few years from now, or decades. I don't know. That's the beauty of life. But I'll be damned if I spend one more time worrying about things I cannot control, getting angry at people who don't deserve my wrath, wishing I had more money so that I could by more things, avoiding the opportunities to give back, and rushing around without cause or reason. My goal is to truly ride the ride of life. To be a survivor of circumstance, and to impart what little wisdom I have acquired thus far onto others. Some can agree, and others are just as equally allowed to disagree with my perspective. But for me, life can be something that people do not fear. Life can be filled with ups and downs that are not necessarily a struggle, but more so a challenge. A challenge to become better, or a challenge to continue to thrive and develop. A means of exploration both inside and out. Life can be a happy adventure.

Chapter 19

Portugal: Beauty by Day, Death by Night

I absolutely love to travel. I have been fortunate enough to get many opportunities to do so. I have lived for years in Asia and in Europe and have visited countries around the world. One such place is Portugal. While living in Spain this beautiful country was approximately a four-hour drive away. Amazing, right? Well, as it turns out, it was a bit more scarring than I had ever imagined.

It started out like any other trip away from the comforts of one's home. Travel, as much as I used to love it, is now taxing on me. I get tired when riding in a car and flying seems to take it out of me more. Nevertheless, I put up with it because I find extraordinary growth in exploring foreign things. Culture, religion, history, and music being a large part of the exploration potential. Following a decent ride, and some utter confusion, we managed to find the place we were looking for, our Airbnb studio apartment. It was set up in a gorgeous area, had a pool, and an amazing view from our balcony. We quickly took to exploring the many things the area had to offer by going to a nearby beach, exploring a nearby town, and enjoying a nice meal. We even went food shopping, since our place had a great kitchenette. When we returned to our room we relaxed a bit until night fall, and tried to turn on the AC unit, which we discovered was not operational. We had been warned about the mosquitos by night, and were encouraged to use the AC, but given our situation, we opted to open the windows because the place was hot. Very hot. There was a mosquito net over the bed, so we thought we were safe.

Holy cow have we never been wrong! The first night of three was brutal. I mean so much so, even with the net, that my knees ended up elevated from all the bites. We were brutally assaulted by blood sucking beasts that would not stop attacking and draining us bone dry. We both must have woken up about five or six times that night. There was a point in the middle of the night my husband woke me up to tell me there were cats. Being that he harbors ill will towards any cat other than our own, I told him they were outside, and that it was fine. I suggested he go back to sleep, but he insisted upon us surveying the apartment just to make sure, because he was sure they were fighting inside. So, I obliged, got up, and in the dark told him that nothing was there. He did not buy it. We turned our attention to the doorway, after he pointed at it and walked to the other end of the room, and sure enough there was a yellow tabby that I did not recognize. It was hissing. So, I walked towards it, while maintaining a reasonable distance (I have been damaged by cats before), and chased it out of the apartment, and off the balcony. I then tried to return to the bed, but John yet again insisted there was another one. Sitting on a chair nearby, in the kitchenette area. I went to take a look, and sure enough, there was another cat sitting there purring. Purring, despite being antagonized by another cat. I picked it up, figuring it was not going to cause any damage, and placed it outside a different entrance. I then returned to bed as my husband did the same, while telling me I was crazy to willingly pick up the second cat. I explained that it had been keeping me company the day before when I was on the balcony, and was also purring, despite the obvious conflict the other cat had initiated. He did not seem convinced, but we returned to bed. We had left the net opened when dealing with the cats, like the sleep deprived geniuses we are, so we experienced even more trauma during the latter half of the night.

We were not prepared for much the next day. Between trading the bed space for naps, we did not get much accomplished on our first full day. We did get out a bit but had little to no energy to deal with life, at that point. We also stayed near the place so that we could touch base with the landlords to see about getting the AC fixed. To our dismay, they were nowhere to be found. So, before dark I spent about an hour and a half with a fly swatter in each hand, killing off the hundred or so mosquitos that had managed to survive the night. At first it was entertaining, but after finding a few hiding spots, and realizing the sheer number of tiny enemies, I had little to no hope for the upcoming night. Neither did my husband, and we both agreed that surviving a third night was practically impossible. Even with the air conditioning fixed. When nightfall hit, I put my husband in bed, and immediately closed the netting, opened the doors, and ran to the safety of the mosquito net. Since we were in a double bed and my husband is over six-foot-tall, the net did not stay closed for long. Although I was already asleep by the time the net was opened by my husband's foot, he got the brunt force of the ensuing attack from a second echelon of blood suckers. He eventually got up and gave in to the borage. I managed to grab his blanket in my sleep and wrap it around my head as soon as he left the bed, because I had felt movement and started to wake. I realized there were mosquitos everywhere, so in an effort to save additional body parts from the feeding frenzy, I used one blanket to surround my face, and the other to cover my body. This worked, until my husband tried to come back to bed, but couldn't. After all, I had stolen the blankets - guess that's my revenge for the nights he took mine! He ended up sleeping on the couch and by morning was quite displeased by the events of the night, so I soon came to discover. Even though we had already decided to throw in the towel he was more than ready to leave.

When I woke up that morning, I was severely startled. I sat up abruptly, and the first words out of my mouth immediately followed. "What happened?", came out of my mouth quicker than my brain could catch up. I found my husband sitting on the couch, with a silly grin on his face. As so many times before, he looked at me like I had a unicorn growing out of my head. He answered by asking me what I was trying to discern, but my mental capacity had not yet caught up with the fact that I was alive, I had survived, and that I was awake, fully drenched in my own sweat. I guess when you are a living heater two blankets can cause you to sweat. I replied by telling him I had no idea and got up to use the restroom. As I entered the bathroom, I realized the enemy was all over the walls and ceiling of the bathroom. I told them out loud that if they stayed where they were, they would survive. I used the bathroom, killed about ten in the process, and walked to the mirror and sink, to wash my hands. It was then that I realized I was staring back at what could only be described as medusa. I had hair in so many twists and tangles that I hardly recognized the person staring back at me. My hair was so contorted that I had managed to make miniature dreads overnight. Since my hair was shorter than shoulder length at the time, every group of strands stuck straight out of my head. I started laughing, realizing that this was the explanation for my husband's curious look. As I tried to unravel the mess, I quickly realized there was no hope. That I was going to have to shower, just to get the knots out with conditioner. My husband waited for me to get done showering, we quickly packed our things, as I stated repeatedly how much I loathed Portugal, that I would sooner die than return, and that this was the last time we would ever be using Airbnb. I left a message for the owner of the place, since they were still nowhere to be found, and made sure they knew the AC wasn't working. After running a few errands that I waited impatiently to finish, we were back on the road. I tried sleeping again, now that I looked halfway presentable in public, but I found myself too angered by the experience and the fact that I literally itched all over and was discovering new wounds every moment we were driving, that I quickly gave up. My husband was also just as relieved to be on the road, and although he had been bit a lot, he had not been bitten nearly as much as me. He also had not realized the severity of the damage my body sustained. I believe he called me a trooper and a true warrior when he saw my knees and the back of my arms for the first time. When we were approaching the border from Spain and Portugal, we pondered what it would be like to acquire the Welcome to Spain just as a personal slight against the country of Portugal. After all, it would be a reminder of my appreciation for home. I was simply under the impression from then on, that I never wanted to leave Spain again. Ever.

Chapter 19.5

The Art of the Bullfight

Bullfighting season follows Feria Season, in Espana. The start of this season occurs in one town, every year, with a running of a bulls opportunity. Needless to say, this is a spectacle that can get out of hand quite quickly. Anyone with a red sash has trained for substantial periods in how to remain safe while luring bulls into the bullring. All others are probably drunk, and usually end up in sticky situations that could be life threatening. It is definitely something to watch, and only watch. Participating in it would be significantly ill advised. There is a planned route that is cordoned off, and if all goes well, no one gets gored during the process. That said, there is little anyone can do about the odd soul who believes they have what it takes to lead a bull in the appropriate direction, without ending up in trouble.

Bulls are incredibly intelligent beasts. Bullfights are an art form that dates back centuries in this area, but not every Spaniard enjoys them. Make no mistake, they are bloody and at times you may feel a certain level of sensitivity for the bulls, but do not show it. The goal is a fifteen-minute race against time, for the matador and his - rarely a her - team to complete a series of stages. There are three. Each stage involves spearing the bull, and if done properly, the bull will fall to its knees before the completion of the final stage. As I mentioned earlier, it is a race against time because bulls learn what is the true target. Although they may initially believe a cape is the target, they will soon learn the goal is to get the matador instead.

Traditionally, there are a couple different bullfights that are available. The first and possibly the most artistic occurs with the matador on horseback. Have no fear, the horses involved are fully protected and have trained around bulls before. For these fights the bull's horns are also shaved down so in the off chance the bull makes contact with the horse, the horse is not gored. The second variation occurs when the matador is on foot. In both scenarios, the goal is to get as close to the bull as possible, and to keep it involved in what you are doing, when appropriate. Certain bulls from selected ranches are chosen, and they are bred for participating in these events. The line of the breed is particularly aggressive, and prices for seats will fluctuate depending upon the cost. The price will also vary depending upon the matador. Young men train for years, since their childhood, to become acclaimed in status. The royals who evaluate the performances will provide each successful matador with an ear, two ears, or two ears and a tail. If anyone earns the rare privilege of receiving the tail, their name in this industry is made. Prices will soar.

If a matador is gored during this display, and is unable to return to the stadium, the bull will survive. The owners will return to the ranch and kill the bull's mother because the meat has already been promised to someone in the community. In addition, the public believes that since the mother created a bull who was capable of achieving such heightened acclaim, she will never be able to do so again. Therefore, while the bull is permitted to live out its days in peace, the mother takes its place as a sign of respect. These spectacular demonstrations of unique artistry are in every way their own culture. Once you enter a bullring, it is imperative to know what every noise and symbol means. There are white flags, whistles, oohs and aahs. Each with their own meaning, depending upon the situation. So, if one can handle the sight of blood, and the highly plausible killing of six bulls, it is worth the experience.

Following this season, there is a break. The tourists return home, and life as you know it continues in Spain.

Chapter 20

The Past that Haunts

My past serves a purpose. Although most would probably not admit that to anyone, this I know for certain. Many people mistake me for cocky, arrogant, even egotistical at times. But one thing is for damn sure. I have too many demons keeping me humble, for that to be the case. The reason I know this is I am not always as strong as I let on in public. I probably have more skeletons in my closet than the average person. Yet I keep pushing past them. Past the individual I once was to ensure I don't allow that pain and suffering to return to my life. The old saying, "it isn't when you're going through crisis that matters, it's what you do with it afterwards" is a motto that I have lived by for years. I have somehow managed to turn negatives into a growing experience and try and find the positive (mostly sarcasm) out of every opportunity. I trust that keeping an open mind, and remaining not necessarily optimistic, but hopeful about the future is what has kept me alive for all these years.

Though we all have experienced some degree of tragedy, I know, some have been through more than others. I have always had faith that we are tested to our breaking point not just to make us stronger, but to build us when we least thought it possible. Some find this through physical accomplishments found through confidence courses. Others discover themselves through surviving strife and the past, reassessing perspective and moving forward with a positive outlook. For me, years of depression, suicide attempts, adoption, abuse, and everything 2016 handed me has been my motivation. With a relatively new diagnosis of PTSD, this has brought me to the realization that it is okay to feel emotions. This happens as a natural process of the human condition. Yet every time I get triggered, there is doubt. Doubt that I cannot make it through this next fiasco, this next challenge. After being relatively exhausted over the years, with regards to emotional strength, this has always been a worry for me. That one day I will give in and give up. There are wounds I will always carry with me. I might be blessed with an attractive face, be white, female, and strong, but all that pales in comparison to the hidden thoughts and feelings that I feel on a daytoday basis.

I used to think feeling emotions was a curse. I've always managed to keep an open perspective of the entire picture, so as to better understand the why's of our actions, assignments, jobs, purpose, etc. While I've always held onto the purpose of helping other people, sometimes I forget to help myself. Most of the time I realize after it is too late that I have burdened myself to the point of weakness, and that is when I am least available to others to provide support. Though everyone needs down time, sometimes understanding when that relaxation is most needed, is the essential part that is missing. Someone can mediate, which I personally do, or reiterate positive messages to themselves over and over again, but setting boundaries for themselves is the most beneficial practice of all.

Recently I have had friends who have felt bad for another individual. They took personal guilt in situations out of their control. Yet I felt nothing. It isn't that I'm a cold-hearted bitch, but none of the people talking were in a position where we let that individual down. We did not inspire the actions that led to her being told no. Nor were we in a position to tell her no. That was a decision repeatedly made on her part. As I explained, setting the restrictions for guilt and responsibility can benefit one's mental health to the nth degree. Setting boundaries for what one can handle in relationships is also key to daily success. Since we are social creatures, despite my attempts to be successful living alone for the majority of my life, I have come to realize that we all have things we allow, and things we cannot abide. Each person varies, and I'm sure environmental factors come into play when making this call, just as emotional and biological factors do too. Yet this is never something anyone can decide for you and taking power back by establishing these limits can significantly improve your lifestyle.

Understanding that no one is perfect and you will frequently experience the breaking of your personal boundaries is something to recognize as well. Again, it is not the challenges that we grow from, but how we use them to our advantage. Handling a situation with immediate violence may work in the immediate future, but if you have any degree of morals, there will be guilt following those actions. If not, you are denying yourself honesty. That is part of the reason why I have spent many years understanding conflict negotiations and mediation. Before getting violent, employing those tactics is how I've managed to find personal growth. Maybe others can learn from that. Over the years, I have experienced the aforementioned guilt. Severely, even. It has plagued me even when I have implemented other tactics before resorting to anything physical. This could be natural, or it could be a sign that I had not set up personal boundaries with regards to finding appropriate guilt and responsibility yet. Although it definitely is one of the factors that got me to such a conclusion. That understanding true responsibility and owning it can not only be the healthiest step to make, but it is also the most challenging.

Owning one's responsibility is something that comes with significant personal strength. I was not always capable of owning up to my actions. And some chose not to embark on this task. To each their own, right? I cannot say one way or the other whether my way is the "right" way or the only way, I just know that it has worked for me thus far. I have found over time that while this can be the most painful task of all, you rely on your positive attributes to get you through the moments of doubt and selfassessment. Reality is the most brutal bitch of all. Let's be honest. Yet if honesty and reality were not hard to endure, they would not be as beneficial as they are. After all, anything worth doing is never easy to accomplish.

During my undergraduate years I spent a semester abroad in Northern Ireland studying conflict resolution and mediation tactics. Not only did I spend the typical time taking classes, but I also spent time with organizations who were perceived as neutral, working to help bridge the gap between Unionists and Nationalists. The common misconception about the historic conflict between Britain and Northern Ireland is that it is a religious war. This is not so. In fact, the conflict stems from generations back when Britain invaded Ireland and claimed its lands. The Republic of Ireland has declared itself uninvolved over recent years and is considerably more safe than the north, and meanwhile there are generations upon generations growing up in the northern part of Ireland who are being taught hate following the death and demise of a brother, cousin, sister, father, uncle, grandparent, niece or nephew. Seeing as there are usually a considerable number of family members in one household, it would appear that everyone knows someone who has personally lost a relative over this long dispute. My job was to help and learn as much as I could about how to bridge the gap between these younger generations that were being taught to hate.

I worked with a group that used environmental work as a mechanism for unity. This included planting trees, organizing school performances, building playgrounds, etc. Through the development of nature and art forms, and also social interaction, children from both sides of the conflict were able to realize that they liked and disliked some of the same things. Another group I worked with was a religious organization that also provided after school events for kids, book clubs and gardening clubs for parents, and religious services that were not geared towards Catholicism or Protestantism. These two religions are frequently affiliated as the cause of the conflict, as I mentioned earlier, but it need not be the reason two people cannot unite over faith. Demonstrating once again that there are similarities on both sides of the conflict that is not determined by political or religious affiliation.

This semester was by far my best semester. I not only enjoyed the opportunity to travel to Europe and see Ireland, which I believe is part of my heritage, but I also got to learn the importance of language for the first time. As a kid, my parents always told me I should become a lawyer because I had a way with words when I wanted to, and to me, this was the beginning of an even more solid approach to manipulating a scenario in my favor! Don't get me wrong, I wasn't always great at it, but with time I learned when I could use words rather than fists to solve a problem. I also have to admit that I did not always work words for entirely moral purposes, but as I grew older, I got tired of those ways and opted to change some things for the better.

Nevertheless, between my certification with the FBI in Basic Crisis Negotiation training and mediation classes in Northern Ireland, I felt like the world was my oyster. I had researched how the women's movement and the civil rights movement in the United States had also sparked movements within Ireland. I learned how those movements started to suggest that there were things people on either side of a conflict could agree on. This was the beginning of my thought process behind getting to develop the philosophy that we can learn from diversity. That we need not all agree on one thing or another in order to be friends, but that instead, a variety of perspectives can be put together to form endless opportunities.

Chapter 20.5

Reality Check

Anyone who has ever experienced a significant life event that has them laid up for a few days is bound to have experienced the reality check one's shower will provide them. I have found that increasingly over the years, my shower seems to be my greatest nemesis. Ordinarily I would say this is because of sheer laziness, but unfortunately this is not the case. I have stopped myself from getting ready in the morning, found the nearest seat, sat down and stared directly at the shower and the wall behind the shower or the shower curtain to figure out if I am indeed in need of taking a shower. I ponder the various ways I can skate by without actually having to clean my entire body from head to toe. Thoughts like, "Is a whore bath good enough", or "Can I get away with just washing my hair", or even, "Do I really need to shave my legs?" have all occurred to me while staring blankly into the great off-white abyss. I have never ended up pleased with the result, because nine times out of ten,it is me contemplating whether to shower, while others would have been showered days ago. For me, showering is not a human component that is a necessity when one is feeling ill. Although, a good long shower can frequently help one feel less like crap warmed over. The issue with that is, one must muster the energy needed to defeat the task at hand.

I faced the shower this morning. I had spent the previous day in the ER due to some migraine, vertigo, and stroke chaos, and I woke up thinking that I would be able to make it to work. I was wrong, and was proven so by my shower. I knew it was going to be a feat for the record books, because as soon as I laid eyes on the curtain I had to pull back, my heart sunk. I knew that no matter how hard I tried to live up to the moment, the shower was going to make or break me. And break me it did.

There's something not so therapeutic about having to turn dripping water on, stand under it while rubbing various cleansing products over your body, and then being required to turn around in circles in order to clean off said cleansing products. Never in my wildest dreams did I ever imagine this task being so challenging, either. Goes to show how great at life I really am. But in all honesty, the moment that gets you the most is having to step out of the shower upon completion of this sorted ritual, while simultaneously maintaining your balance. Especially when you know you were way too weak to even begin to consider the task of showering, and instead you should have just given up long before you started.

I spent the remainder of the day in bed, sleeping, after my shower this morning. Mind you, I spent more than 13 hours asleep the night before. I can honestly say I don't ever remember being able to get remotely close to that much sleep, without being severely inebriated. Nevertheless, I had every intent on making it to work, but the shower defeated me once again. So, in my bright mind, the shower seems to be the most fitting reality check available to the human being, when they are feeling bigger and better than they actually are.

Chapter 21

Pain

Anyone who lives with chronic pain understands the struggle of the next person with similar issues. For those who don't have to undergo this battle, here's a little glimpse into the life of someone who has lived with pain on and off for years. The first thing to know is that pain is exhausting. Daily pain is even worse. After suffering from degenerative disc disease and severe headaches and migraines for years, I can tell you first-hand that there is nothing more exhausting than waking up in the morning and feeling as though you have been hit by a ton of bricks. I spent almost six years, on and off, on narcotic pain medications until the right procedure was found which helps relieve my pain so much so that I no longer require medication. I still get migraines, and usually they cluster together for a couple weeks to a month, and then go away for a period. And require medicine to help me with that, but for the time being at least, I am pain free. And what a relief it is.

Pain also comes in other forms, however. This is the side that not many people have the courage to discuss in public. Depression is pain. Feeling inadequate is pain. And after a while these negative thoughts about oneself wear you down to the point where you doubt you can get back up. Having been in this situation many times before I can tell you that the chemical imbalance that occurs in the brain to cause this predicament is real. Medication has proven as much. I have been on a multitude of medicines, in varying doses, over the years to try and help me. I have also been taken off of medicines for periods of times as well, when things were going well. One thing that I know beyond any shadow of doubt is suffering alone is not an option.

When you feel as though you cannot make it another day, and that you have no one out there to help you, because they will never understand what it is you're going through, you still have someone. You have me. There is very little at this stage in my life that I have not already been through. Sexual abuse, check. Emotional abuse, check. Physical abuse, check. Adoption, check. Miscarriage, check. PTSD, check. Abandonment, check. All of these things make a person stronger, in some ways, but they can also make them more vulnerable. This vulnerability, however, may not be visible. It will be internal, and other than the person who is feeling it having the courage to work through it within their head, there is not much else anyone else can do but be present. That is perhaps the most challenging thing about knowing someone with a psychological struggle. Nevertheless, that does not mean anyone is alone.

By standing by someone's side you are demonstrating a show of force. That you will not let that person fail. That that person means the world to you, enough that you will be by them no matter how hard they try to push you away. With kids, this is a very popular technique because they want to see how far you will go to demonstrate your loyalty to them. Sometimes older folks do the same thing. There is not a person in the world that will go through everything you have gone through, because that's just not how it works. Yet having support means that while someone may not get exactly what you're struggling with, they will still pick up the phone, or come hear you out, or visit with you when you're feeling lonely.

Loneliness was my biggest issue for years. I thought I was going to die as an ugly cat lady that no one realized had died, until after the stench got so bad that someone had to notice. I remember actually sitting in my apartment shortly before I started dating my husband crying because I thought my cats would eat my face because no one would be there to feed them, and I would be unidentifiable. I'm not joking! Irrational, right? Nevertheless, it was how I felt. And in that moment, I went from one irrational thought to validating it with everything I knew about myself before then. Because I had been adopted and abandoned as a kid I was doomed to remain alone for the rest of my life. Because I did not get along all that well with my adoptive parents who raised me over the last couple of years, I would end up alone. And that is how my mind works at times. I may know exactly how ludicrous every assumption or correlation is at the time, but it doesn't matter. I still worry.

Over time I have gotten over the loneliness thing. In fact, now I love being alone. That's when I do my best writing. In the middle of the night when no one's awake and the cat prefers to sleep on the pillow next to my computer desk, that's when I'm the best at what I do. It's quiet. I can focus. I'm not distracted by my deathly case of squirrel syndrome. There are no lights, cars, noises to pull me away from my thought process, and I have learned to embrace the things I once hated about myself. And truly, that is the way out of any crisis. To face it head on and to know that no matter how terrible you might feel at your lowest point, there's always going to be a way up from there.

For anyone living with someone fighting the physical or psychological fight, you have to know that despite all efforts, a person in one or more of these conditions is just worn down. It may take them a while to get out of their low phase. It also may take them a while to hit rock bottom. But like anything well done, it is done at one's own pace. You cannot rush genius, just as much as you cannot rush one's ability to process through an event or series of events that led to their current predicament. This is why everyone embraces the rags to riches mentality. Someone who was a former Army Ranger getting hit by an IED, for example, and having to recover after losing a limb, or two, or three. Watching that person get back on top and having control over their life again is one of those addictive pleasures that the media feeds off of, for positive and inspirational stories. Yet, the struggle is only truly felt by those who have had to experience it for themselves. We may highlight it for the public and pat a guy or gal on the back for a job well done, but that kudos is only momentary. Immediately after the spotlight falls away, they are just another person anyone may pass by and sneer at for having a physical deformity.

The same is true for those with psychological issues. You never know what is going on inside someone else's brain, until you have been there. Unfortunately, that's not possible. Which is just another reason why I prefer that the only way to truly love yourself, is to give everyone else the benefit of the doubt. Do not rush to judgement because someone else tells you one thing or another. Do not believe a media story just because of what they have presented to you. Read the facts, do your independent research and find out what you can personally before coming to a conclusion. Because you may find that the story is completely different than what has been presented on a larger screen.

Chapter 22

Sexual Expression

Who does not love sex? I mean really? Men think about it all the time, and women do too. Whether or not they are willing to admit it is another thing, but in all seriousness, sex is, and can be, amazing! Without going into the usual melodrama about sexual expression and how it varies depending upon gender, I will admit this, I am a very different person than I was years ago with regards to sexual expression! Some people who know me from my college days, for example, may think of me in one light, that varies drastically from who I have become in the years since. But sexual expression does not have to be limited to what one feels inside. Expressing oneself through actions with another partner can be the most beneficial and stress relieving outlet, if given the opportunity to be utilized.

I think marketing in this day and age has been transformed into sexual innuendos and phallic objects, which has made sex something that is seemingly okay for all ages. In the millennial generation, kids of eleven are getting on birth control. And here I got my first kiss on my 16th birthday! Children are having children, and that is far from okay. Even at 32, I'm not sure I am capable of raising a kid because I barely know what I'm doing half the time. Which, ironically, is how most parenting goes, but this in no way justifies the notion that children should be violating their innocence and youth that early on. It is my belief that they should be enjoying their younger years and growing up doing kid things, and eventually learning about themselves and about sexual expression in a much more gradual form.

By allowing ourselves to foster the images of casual sex and physical nudity in everything from Burger King advertisements to condom commercials, we are essential invalidating the fundamentals of what marriage and companionship truly is. The bond that is formed through a one-night stand may be liberating, yet it does not make for a sound depiction of whether or not you can stand an individual. That being said, I'm not going to sit here and say one-night stands are bad, by any means. That would admittedly be hypocritical, but what I do mean is that there is less emphasis on the importance of knowing a person, and the fundamentals that marriage or commitment requires. Friendships are hard enough to maintain over the years. I only have one or two friends that I still talk to from twenty years back. Literally. That kind of undying loyalty and dedication to keep in touch with someone that long takes a kind of acceptance that jumping into bed with someone after a first date cannot foster. And that's even assuming you go on a first date!

I think the bottom line is that this marketing ploy to give people what they want and to manipulate the customer into being sucked into a TV show, or game because of a physical characteristic or sexual component undermines the quality of what sex can be. The stereotypes portrayed of those who enjoy less conventional forms of sex are also harmful. Not only do they frequently mislead the public, but they can also get people in over their heads.

I once had a friend's son, who was a bit older than me, assume that because I was playing pool with his father repeatedly in the same night, that I was trying to court him. The son told me that he would never call me "mom". I just looked at him and laughed. Later on that night he approached me again and admitted that he had been wrong, and that after watching me interact and talking to me some more he realized that I had no such intentions. I thanked him and reassured him that I had no desire to become a family member. And from there, somehow the conversation shifted to BDSM. Don't ask me how, because I don't have the foggiest, but it did. This guy proceeded to tell me that BDSM was about physical violence and aggression and that it was only the sadistic who could get off on something like that. And I immediately told him that I disagreed. Not that I have had much experience in that world, if any at all, but to me it seems more like a vulnerability fetish or power play that is involved in the BDSM world. Where you learn to trust one person, like no other. Where you both get to know the ins and outs of that individual so well, that you would allow them to do things any other person off the street would never be able to.

I recently talked to another friend about this notion of vulnerability and submission. About being able to give trust in another person and sharing a level of intimacy that only you are privy to having access to. And it is those connections that seem to make lasting relationships. I'm not saying that everyone needs to be involved in some type of BDSM relationship in order to be successful at a marriage or commitment, by any means. But if anything, I almost feel as though intimacy and personal connection have drifted out of sexual expression, out of marriages, out of relationships in general. Because if you are jumping into bed with someone right off quick, and not getting to know them first, and then assuming you will be involved in a relationship that will last a lifetime, then maybe you are believing a fairytale. I will say that there are some who can date and get married a few months later and last a lifetime. But to be truly intimate with someone, and to truly value them as a person, one must stop marketing themselves as sexual objects and start taking the steps towards expression through sexual identity.

A different friend decided to kidnap me once for a field trip, and didn't tell me where we were going, until it was too late. A sex shop, she said. She wanted me to help her pick out a pleasure instrument. Why she thought I would be good for this, I don't know. But this was not my first time being in this predicament, shockingly enough. Yet somehow as I was discussing the pros and cons of knowing the mission before being dragged to the shop, I also admitted that maybe I wasn't the best person to help someone else figure out what they found pleasurable. Nevertheless, it was this topsecret experience that no one was supposed to know about. I thought to myself, why? Why is this so embarrassing? This is an innovative couple who is willing to think outside the box in order to keep themselves faithfully committed. And yet, there seems to be a level of shame attached to shops like these. That this acknowledgement that toys exist to stimulate pleasure are filthy, when in fact, they can really help a marriage! I know that seems impossible, but I have had friends who are in love with people, have been with them for years, but have not been sexually satisfied. Why should anyone feel shame if they are trying to improve and enjoy themselves while having sex?

This is the reality that so many people live in these days. Sex was never talked about in my home, when growing up. My uncle was the first person to talk to me about sex, actually. I was staying at my aunt and uncle's house for a summer, and I met a boy. You know the story from there. We hit it off and before you knew it my guardians were pulling me off to the side to discuss how it was ill advised to go home with any unwanted diseases, or an unexpected package due to arrive in nine to ten months. Nevertheless, me being me, I simply explained that I had no issues going to the store, if need be. That everything was fine and that I was not doing all that, considering I had just met the guy. I was young and innocent then, so the thought of having anything less than a relationship had never occurred to me. Nevertheless, as time grew on, I started to recognize that maybe sex wasn't as dirty as it was portrayed. With all the scantily clad women, and the media displaying phallic objects, maybe it wasn't something to be ashamed of, despite the public perception. As I grew into my 20's I started exploring that world. Most of the time I was too lazy to deal with the relationship aspect, so friends with benefits was my thing. Plus, all I was focused on back then was a career so I didn't want to get tied down in a relationship that would make me struggle to make life-defining choices. Instead, I wanted to be "free". So, free I was.

The bad thing about friends with benefits relationships is that someone always ends up falling in love. Admittedly, I have broken many hearts because usually it wasn't me doing the falling. But something I did notice, was that sex was something I enjoyed. It was a level of private expression between me and another. It did not need to be discussed in public. It needed not to be something that anyone necessarily knew about. But it was an intimate connection between you and whomever you chose. There was a time that I was more promiscuous than others, don't get me wrong, but I valued every experience for what it was. It was art. It was expression. It was exploration, of self and another. And I think in this day and age that exploration is a moot point. Sex can really be a beautiful thing, even if not done within the traditional confines of marriage (for the old-school religious folks). Yet, with the boost in technology I feel as though personal connections are not what they used to be, and that changes how people engage sexually.

Some may also see what is being done in the media and on television and think that those interactions should be what happens in real life. But to do that is almost to limit oneself. The porn industry is probably another huge influence in the lives of many with regards to their sexuality, because they see how things are portrayed, and are more than likely to mimic the actions of that person. For me personally, I just want to enjoy the experience. I have spent many hours going over things in my head, debating and eventually understanding my sexuality, and it isn't easy. It wasn't easy as a teenager, to figure out what was going on with my body, especially in a house that didn't really talk about sex much, and it wasn't easy to figure out how to be "right" with the enjoyment of the experiences I had. Everything else was telling me sex was to be done within a marriage, or on a movie screen, but certainly not by me. In order to be right with my feelings, I had to admit to myself, that I was different. I am not the next person, just as much as they are not me. So, having my own wants and desires was something to further delve into, and it became clear that I needed to figure out what I wanted out of life. If that included sexual expression, great! If not, also great! I cannot tell anyone else how to live their lives, and I don't expect they will ever successfully change mine.

Chapter 23

Religion & Politics

What sarcastic writer wouldn't include a chapter of their book entitled Religion and Politics!? Honestly, these are two topics, out of three, that are not supposed to be discussed on a first date (or probably ever), so why not include them here!? Honestly, because this is one of those forbidden topics. And, if you have not picked up on this yet, I am a bit of a self-defined rebel! Nevertheless, both of these categories are important conversational pieces, and you can either disagree or agree with my perspective, and I will harbor no ill will.

I grew up attending religious services as a kid. I sang in the church choir, attended Sunday School, and was by all accounts religious. Nevertheless, I was unaware of what was actually being said, because I was too young to understand the message of the sermons each Sunday. As we moved from place to place over the years, I was exposed to many different forms of Christianity and attended a variety of services. One might frown upon this, but it opened my eyes considerably to the multitude of choices. It actually may have overwhelmed me, in hindsight. One thing I could never reconcile is why people had to have their own brand of religion. Why this was something everyone took so seriously and didn't seem to mimic the messages portrayed in the Good Book.

This was the first time I recognized hypocrisy within the human form. I didn't understand how a Christian could call themselves accepting of others and devout, yet hate another because of the color of their skin, their race, gender, religious preference, etc. I also didn't understand why more people didn't act the way they preached. For me, it was pretty clear. If you say you will do something, you do it. If you read a religious text that tells you to not harbor anger towards another, you don't. Going to a service each week doesn't make you more or less likely to be a Christian. And nine times out of ten, I found those who were religious service attendees were the most heinous people I had ever met. Sometimes, they were downright evil. For those who had a more nontraditional approach to religion, and didn't feel the need to attend weekly services, they usually acted the way I expected Christians to act. As with most things, there's always one or two that stray from the common perception or mold, but for the most part, this still remains true even in this day and age, in my experience.

It is hard to say that religion has influenced populations for good, when there is a standard ignorance among people with regards to other religious perspectives. I was lucky enough to grow up in an area that had Christians, Muslim, Hindu, and Buddhists. I never had a problem with anyone. Sure, their ceremonies and religious rites were different than mine, but I respected them. I would travel to Borobudur just to see the huge man-made statues and experience the aura that surrounded the place. I would travel to temples and done headgear not because I had to, but because I wanted to be respectful of the religious specifications that varied from mine. I would light candles inside various religious temples and attend Bat Mitzvahs for my friends. All of this was normal for me. So, when I started noticing the behaviors of people to the left and right of me, I began to see that traditional religion was not for me. Attending services doesn't make me more devout. It doesn't make me more spiritual or capable of trying to live a Christian life. Instead, I just aim to be the best person I can be. I keep my head down, help when I can, make decisions based upon a strong moral standing, and do the best that I can do. If I step out of bounds, because no one's perfect, I give myself a talking to. And I police myself up, meaning, I make sure there's recognition in place for how to better change my actions the next time. And I make amends whenever I can. Morality is my religion.

How ironic that one can end one section with the start of another - morality. Politics is always one of those things that focuses more on perception versus reality. This is something they talked a lot about in the military when I was there. Now, I see it entranced throughout the criminal justice system, and throughout the United States' political realm. It also exists within the world arena as well. Everyone wants to put their best face forward. Unfortunately, that usually means something has got to give. Usually that something is morality.

Choosing the hard right over the easy wrong is never anyone's favorite thing to do, and it can be quite humbling. I believe the ability to do this is a major defining component in someone's character. To open a dialogue, discuss and possibly apologize to someone for doing them wrong is essential to the quality of person you are. Being able to stomach making amends without expecting anything in return is also hard. It is rewarding, if you let it, but hard, nonetheless. All too often in politics, I see people deciding that it is best for everyone if the truth is not divulged. Take the war on drugs, for example. The US has funded crusade after crusade against drugs, yet the only thing we have to show for after decades of this battle is devastation. Devastation to homes, farms, other countries, families, etc. We have gone into other places and systematically destroyed the lives of many who cannot afford to start over. All with the hope that we will end up with fewer drugs on the streets. Unfortunately, it is a never-ending battle. We cannot win. It is unreasonable to think that drugs are going to stop being used by people, just as much as its unreasonable to think all crime will cease if we just do this or that. Making goals that are realistic can at times be the hardest thing to do.

There are other world events that I have questioned over the years. Countries invading other countries in order to gain land and loot or pillage to improve their circumstances. While I understand everyone has to live somehow, I do not believe that doing it at another's expense is the way to go. When the British sent over the folks to discover what became known as the US, they systematically destroyed an entire population. An entire culture. Native Americans were not aggressive. There were some tribes that were more so than others, but we literally landed and invaded. If someone did that to us in this day and age, we would do what we had to in order to survive, dollars to donuts. So, tell me, are we really in the right?

There are a multitude of critics surrounding the terrorist movement. Some people believe we should not engage with them, and we should be peaceful and try to come to an understanding. Others believe that we should have gone in and destroyed them a long time ago. Yet the political climate within the world dictates these plans now more than ever. We can say they are the bad guys, and truth be told I would agree with that. Yet, these are also people who have suffered immensely. It's not just that they have lost family members, or that they live in a third world country that has been destroyed by a war that has waged in one way or another for years. It isn't just that they want something more for themselves or believe in the ideology of a few. In fact, if anything, my master's research has taught me that the average person who straps a bomb to his or her chest, is just like you or me. They have been convinced and manipulated into believing that sacrificing themselves is a just cause. They have been convinced that their sacrifice is a religious act, when in fact it is anything but. The struggle of these entry-level members within the terrorist movement is incredibly real, and just like inner city gangs in the US, terror leaders and recruiters seek them out. They seek out the unsupervised, the impressionable, and they slowly integrate religion into their lives, comradery, and then they begin asking things of an individual. If they want to stand true to the community they just found versus the lonely life they led before, who wouldn't decide to do some small task for the religious leader? They are very seldom aware of what it is they are actually doing, with regards to the bigger picture. Can you really fault them for embracing their humanistic nature and wanting companionship? Wanting to belong to something? Can you fault a freshly initiated gang member for joining a group because he or she has been incarcerated for some crime and found themselves unprotected? Granted the strategies of these terror or gang leaders is all wrong, and hopefully one day an individual might live to acknowledge or see that, but the harsh reality is that that is not likely. It is more likely that unless they have something to offer, they are just another member.

So how does this relate to US politics, one might ask? I'll tell you. No one wants to be seen on a universal scale destroying people who have already lived through the death of their entire family, and have been more or less brainwashed by zealots who claim their mission is religion. Realistically, the people worth destroying are the leaders, the teachers, the recruiters of the terror or gang movement. Everyone else is just a pawn in a real-life game they don't have the clarity or insight to understand. So, how do you justify killing a large group of people who are just as culpable as the rest of them, yet are somehow innocent to the degree to which they have been brainwashed? How do we close a facility like Guantanamo Bay, Cuba, and expect countries to willingly welcome those who have been deemed approved for release, when they have been imprisoned for good reasons? They have been proven in one way or another to be repeatedly in the wrong place at the wrong time. At this point, had they been truly innocent, they would not be part of the 60-some detainees left in those detention facilities. We literally waged war against one group, only for another to pop up and claim dominance. Politics is combating the never-ending evil that exists in the world, but doing so in a way that makes you look innocent.

The United States has all too often been perceived as the hero, and the villain. The Vietnam War and Korean Wars were the start to manipulation of the press. The general perception was that the US was somehow worse than the people we were fighting, and our country bought into that. Our citizens bought into the strife that war caused and blamed our nation for it. I believe that despite the need to remove strategic members of terror groups and gangs, we are at a loss when we are considering how to do so, while remaining publicly appreciated, and how to prevent another snake head from appearing. Realistically speaking, war doesn't breed positivity though. There is always destruction, death, and negativity. There are always going to be family members that lose, people who are displaced, and cities destroyed. That is the reality of war. Yet, somehow we have managed to take most wars to the shores of other countries, so we do not witness the aftermath. It doesn't happen locally. We may see glimpses of it on television, and we say, "how sad", and then forget it two minutes later. It isn't our realityor our circumstance, so there's no need to spend time focusing on it. We may even go so far as to throw money towards some relief group to help refugees (or so we are made to believe), but we are too detached to understand the implications. The generations of strife that has occurred in the Middle East,the constant battle, and the inability to reconstruct by the time another war starts. Be it internal amongst rival groups in a country or initiated by foreign entities.

The harsh reality is that politics is something only certain individuals care about. In order to make things look on the up and up, a multitude of energy, time, and money will be spent. Nevertheless, the battle is never won. There is always someone willing to blame someone else for something and seek revenge. There is always someone who is never going to be happy with an accord. There is always going to be that advocate for a movement that they believe doesn't get enough attention. There will always be conflicts between movements, be it on a national or international scale. There is simply, no way to win. As depressing as that may seem, the truth can hurt. Despite this, our only hope for politics is to avoid it altogether. Is that realistic, probably not. But I pride myself on being the person who can take a stand. Tell someone in a nonaggressive way, ideally, that something may not be as they had hoped. The worst thing you can do in the face of disaster or wrongdoing is to not speak up. If we begin this at an individual level, we may have a chance to solve problems. But remember, it is not necessarily what you say, but how you say it that matters.

~ Chapter 23.33 ~

Clean Up on Aisle 3

The other day I was sitting at home minding my own business, enjoying the quiet time to myself late at night. It was brutally interrupted by a shoot-out. I heard five single gunshots, followed by two double-taps, and about a minute and a half after that five single shots rang out. Being the solid citizen I am, I picked up the phone and dialed 911. Little did I know I was to be insulted. Not once, but twice. The first dispatch attendant picked up the phone after a few rings, and as I explained what I had heard, she asked me if I was sure it was in the area. I was living in a place that had a few different cities all clustered together at the time, and I was sort of taken aback by the question. It is not every day that you get someone calling in to tell people in great detail as to what they witnessed, so I guess I sort of assumed I would be taken seriously. Before my mind could catch up to my mouth, I caught myself saying, "Ma'am, I am an Army Veteran and I can hear the gun shots, and the echoes. I would say it's 300 meters away, give or take". With that, the woman sounded quite surprised and informed me she would connect me to the local dispatcher immediately. This comment only fueled my confusion and curiosity because it is not every day that you call 911 and are directed to a dispatcher that is potentially in another state. Nevertheless, I bit my tongue and thanked her, only to be forwarded to a line that proceeded to ring and ring.

After about 15 rings, a gentleman picked up the phone and proceeded with the usual rigmarole. I proceeded to tell him what I told the other operator and was surprised to receive the same questioning of my expertise and qualifications. Now I was beginning to lose my patience. Again, it is not every day someone can give you an exact number of shots fired, in the sequence they are fired in, and an approximate timeline between each shot. So, I told the operator about my military background and proceeded to explain the situation involving echoes and whatnot. He told me to stay safe, remain in my home, and that police were already in the area patrolling. I thanked him, and said, "While I have you on the line… ". Worst idea ever. I simply wanted to know what my civil rights were in the state I had just moved to, with regards to defending my own home, and as a result my ego got too big for my britches. I received an onslaught of advice about refraining from violence and about allowing the police to do their job, protecting and serving and all that jazz. Of course, this guy had no idea I was a military police officer in a past life (a detail I left out in earlier conversation), but all I had wanted to know was, can I defend myself if someone breaks in, and not worry about going to jail for resorting to violence.

In a past life, I would probably have killed first and then thought later. This year, however, it was specifically an innocent thought that led me awry. What happens if someone breaks in, and I can't talk them out of my home! But my brain has led me astray before and sure as all get-out, it did it again. I got no information I had wanted, and instead I received a lecture. After I hung up, the end of the conversation really got to me. I had waited 15 rings for this guy to pick up the phone, after being transferred from another operator, and to add insult to injury I still didn't know if I could get away with bodily harm of a robber, thief, or break and enterer, if necessary. So, the thought occurred to me, who in their right mind is going to stay on their couch and just pick up the phone (to listen to it ring repeatedly) when someone breaks into their home? Who would do this during the day, let alone at 430am!?! And what am I supposed to do when the operator doesn't pick up after the first ring, and instead gets to me after 15? A lot can happen in the time a phone takes to ring 14 additional times.

So now, I was stuck between a rock and a hard place, while trying to enjoy my renewed silence. I spent a few more minutes pondering the degree of insanity that occurred in the conversations with both operators, and while I understood that they couldn't just encourage independent action, they could have at least told me whether or not I would be liable if someone got hurt by my hand, after breaking into my house. I was forced to resort to independent research in order to get my answer, and for the life of me I'm still not even sure I trust the gibberish that is legal speak anyways. Suffice it to say, I do not recommend calling the police at ass crack early in the morning to report a crime, when you have more important questions that come up as a result of your conversation with them. You will not get your answer.

Chapter 24

Drunken Joy

Oh! How the mighty have fallen! And I'd be lying if I didn't say they were some of the best times in my life. Albeit I probably paid for them with some degree of physical pain or humiliation afterwards, but I guess there's always a price to pay when you're Trouble, with a capital T!

There are just too many ways to go about this, so I guess I'll start with a good college tale. I had a friend, her name is going to be Katie. Katie and I became close and stayed close for most of the duration we were in college. We opted to go to a house party at a mutual friend's house one night but got separated. Before long, I was with a group of people who had no idea where we were going, and I was significantly intoxicated, thinking I knew the way. After about a half hour of walking up and down the same road, trying to find the right street to turn on, Katie came to save the day. She showed me and the others that had depleted in numbers, where to go. And before you know it, we were at our friend's house! We quickly realized we were way too intoxicated for how sober everyone else was, so we decided to make our way back to campus and see what else was going on. However, it occurred to drunk me that it was a prime idea to jump onto Katie, every few steps. Of course, this was back in a day and age where it may not have been appropriate to be publicly intoxicated. Since we were in college, very little actually occurred to us as problematic.

Like, what if the police show up? Or, what if they realize someone is underage and drunk?

Needless to say, none of these things occurred to me, but they did occur to Katie. And as she continuously urged me to cut it out, we were both too busy laughing about it, which I knew was not a good thing. Because that meant, I could continue jumping her, and see how far I could take it. The next morning, I woke up in dire straits. I hurt all over. Had bruises and cuts, and literally had no idea how I managed to make it home. So, I did what any responsible person would do, I called Katie. Before long I was reminded of my antics, and was informed that eventually I got my ass beat. Plain and simple, because apparently when you repeatedly attack your friend who is less sober than you, you suck at defending yourself when they fight back!

Another great thing about my undergraduate school, was that it was a dry campus. It received funding from Quaker entities that required the school be dry, however that did very little to stop us. In fact, we had a branch of the Hash House Harriers present, and I was an avid fan. After hours of drinking in the middle of a Saturday, Saturday nights were even better! After thirteen hours of drinking, what better way to start Sunday than hungover, or if you were lucky, totally still drunk from the night before! For me, this was how I spent my college years. Now that I feel the pain and anguish of defeat every time I sip an alcoholic beverage, I wonder how I ever managed to survive it all.

One night, my friends and I decided it would be great to have a kegger. So, after the inevitable purchase of said beer, and a few drinks, we opted to go for a friendly mosh pit style brawl. I had arrived a little later than everyone else, so I ended up diving onto the pile of bodies, only to be flipped off the top, and wound up headfirst onto a bocce ball. For those who are not aware, a bocce ball is incredibly hard. It is a ball used to play a game that is quite similar to Cricket, but it is by no means something you want to make head contact with. Before long, I realized I had hit something other than the ground and I got the attention of my friends who quickly noticed I was not okay. Some ran inside, while others tried to get me to stop giggling, and to leave the egg that had formed instantaneously on my head, alone. They were not successful. But I did abide by icing my noggin and before long I was in front of a mirror, utterly impressed with the black and blue egg that had become the side of my forehead. I went to the doctor the next day who was not impressed, and he informed me that I was lucky to be alive, because I had received a moderate concussion, and should not have been allowed to sleep the night before. I sort of shrugged it off, and continued on with my life, which entailed playing in a tennis match against a very religious team. At that point in time, my doubles partner's name was Sai Ko Honda. This chick was amazing! She and I were a fabulous pair, but unfortunately, as we were introduced as Silver and Sai Ko, the coach of the opposing team thought this was less entertaining. The guy approached our coach and complained that it was disrespectful to introduce players by their nickname, and when my coach replied that he used our real names, he was forced to show the roster so the other coach would believe him. As entertaining as that was, it was not a fantastic idea for me to be on the court with a still throbbing head. But I thoroughly enjoyed the fact that my hair was incredibly short. This meant that the only way to wear it off my neck was to put it up in two little devil-ear ponytails on the upper sides of my head. Meanwhile I had a goose egg with bruising that had now drifted downward into my entire eye area, and I took full advantage of the experience. I was not afraid to pump my fist and let out mean noises, and before long I had the opponents on the other side of the net shaking in their boots!

If only I could say this was the only time I had gotten a concussion while in college. Sadly, it isn't. I actually got three concussions in one week, a few years earlier. My freshman year we had an old school phone that most kids these days wouldn't recognize. It had a spin dial and a cord that was attached to it. The phone rang one day when my roommate and I were in our room, and I ran over to pick it up. As I said hello, I walked away from the wall, and put the phone between my ear and shoulder. I walked a bit too far, and before I could hear a response, the phone sling-shotted across the room and slammed into the wall. I ran over to it, picked it up, and tried to get a response, to see if whoever had called was still there. No one was there. I looked at my roommate with a huge grin, and we both started laughing. I proceeded to dive onto my bed, but missed the bed and ran head first into the short bookcase that was sitting next to the bed. I got up, laughing even harder, but in considerable pain, and looked at my roommate who proceeded to laugh even harder as well. After a bit we realized my head was bleeding and so we tried to clean it up as best we could, and I was off to tennis practice shortly thereafter. At this point in my life, I had been playing tennis for years. Never, not once, had I ever hit myself in the head with my racket until this day. I not only did it once, I did it multiple times. For the life of me, I still have no idea how. But I laughed it off once again, realizing that I had just hit myself in the same spot that I had hit on the bookcase earlier, and proceeded to finish off the practice being extra careful to avoid my head. Later that night, against all rationale, I was hanging out with some friends. They were drinking, and so was I, but not to my usual extent. I jumped on my roommates back and demanded a piggyback ride, but the way I landed on her made both of us fall down. Of course, she fell backwards on top of me, and you guessed it, I landed headfirst into the hallway wall. The next day I went to the doctor and explained what had happened. I had a massive headache, and a very condescending and unenthusiastic doctor gave me some ibuprofen and told me to keep my head away from hard inanimate objects. I now can see the humor and irony is his statement. Well played asshole doc, well played!

My friend Katie (from earlier in this chapter) got married a few months after I did. This was our first road trip as husband and wife, and it was my first opportunity to see some college friends that I had not connected with for a good seven or eight years. It was an awesome ceremony, with an even better reception at a four or five-star hotel. Needless to say, we had some adult fun, with alcoholic beverages. We ate, caught up, danced, and before long I was ready to leave. I made my way downstairs with my husband, we eventually climbed into the shuttle and went back to the hotel. On the way back I passed out. When we arrived, my husband woke me up, and I barely made it down the shuttle stairs, and over to the side door of the hotel that required key access. My husband had the key, so I waited impatiently for him to open it up, and as soon as I took a step inside, I threw my hands up in the air and screamed, "STAIRS!". I proceeded to climb up said stairs on all fours, and when I made it to the top, I crawled on all fours to our room, which was directly to the right at the top of the stairs. I got on my feet and my husband opened the door of our room, and said, "You're free. Do what you want now that you're in the room". Never in the history of mankind is that a good thing to say to a drunk person. True to form, I sprinted to the bed and jumped onto it with my arms and legs outstretched. What I had failed to calculate was the bed would rebel against my attempts to land in it, and sure enough I bounced off the bed, and into a neighboring TV stand. My husband was less than pleased and immediately put me to bed, against my will. Once again, I woke up the next morning hating life and in excruciating pain. Yet another time I was required to learn about my actions from the person closest to me. As I started laughing, I realized that the humor and fun of the night before was soon to stab me in the back, since I was hating life and we had an eleven-hour car ride to complete.

Chapter 25

Immeasurable Glory

Probably the single most painful experience I have ever had is getting pepper sprayed. There are always certain things you never want to do in a job, and for the Army this was one of those. There are generally three different levels of pepper spray application, however for anyone who works in confinement and may carry or come into contact with the use of pepper spray, you must get sprayed. Makes sense, right? Well, this is the end all be all of hell incarnate. Let me tell you. They spray your forehead, ideally, with a line of pepper spray, and then expect you to run through a course beating things and taking down people, so that in the event you can do this in real life. Let me tell you, if someone sprays me in real life, across the forehead, in a confinement setting, I will not have my eyes open long enough to hit a target. I am more likely to hit anything else but, and be completely unaware that I have missed said target.

Let me explain in detail what this feels like, from my perspective. At first, I was under the impression that it would suck. Quite a reasonable understanding of the experience. One that most would agree with. The level of suck that embraced my world does not even compare to the reality of the moment you are hit. The moment the capsaicin touched my face I believe the first two sentences out of my mouth were, "Oh, this is not cool!" and "God help the soul that makes me use this on them!" There is a newfound understanding of exactly what hell you are raining down on someone when you are required to do it to yourself. It is more or less a sick comic joke to be willing to endure pain, just for the sake of the possibility of coming into contact with it while on the job. Well, let me tell you, if you hit yourself with your own darn can of pepper spray, you're doing it wrong! If someone else near you is hitting you instead of the intended target, they are doing it wrong! This is to say that there is always the possibility that some will rub off on you if you are hands on at any point with someone who has been sprayed. But at no point should someone really be aiming a can of pepper spray at their colleague and telling them to prepare themselves. Usually, the warning is intended for an unruly individual, who is likely more or less on their own at that point. Anyone on a guard force is usually covered up to some degree with protective gear, and so there's always the chance (a really unfortunate chance, mind you) that you can get caught at a bad angle (the wind blew some in the wrong direction, etc.), but more than likely you should not be the primary receiver of the pepper spray blast.

Since pepper spray comes in a multitude of forms, spray versus mist for example, there really is a wide variety of ways you can be exposed, both primary and secondary contact. However, the only time you are really ever in for a treat is when you get sprayed directly on the forehead, or if you are really lucky, in the eyes.

I'm willing to argue that I was sprayed a bit too low, but who knows. Either way, it seeps down your brow into your eyes and it stings. It stings a lot. So much so, that if you are lucky enough to indulge in this "training" in the summer months, the sun on your forehead for the next few hours feel like it's burning a hole through your dome. For the especially lucky ones, they will decide that in order to free themselves of said pain, they will stand in the shower and wash themselves. Well, as we all know, things roll downhill. And I'll be darned if that pepper spray does not decide to light up every living cell on your body with the exact same sensation that just ripped a whole through your forehead, if you do that. This is yet another sick joke attached to the experience. So, usually the trainers will have access to water out on the training grounds. You are supposed to bend over and splash water on your forehead, kind of reminiscent of someone attempting to drink a beer upside down. It never works.

For the most special candidates, you will end up with an eye infection following this experience. I'm not sure why, but there is always one. Guess who was the lucky one, after the first time - yes, first time - I was pepper sprayed! Me! The pain and anguish of having an overly fried egg for a forehead stayed with me for a good two weeks following the training experience. It did not occur to me that maybe I had an infection, which is something you are advised about during the pre-training brief. It just occurred to me that maybe I did not wash all the pepper spray out from my eyeballs. But low and behold, eventually I gave in and went to the doctor who very quickly diagnosed me with an infection and gave me some drops and possibly some other oral stuff. It is God's sick joke to have to turn around and put drops into your fired-up eyeballs, in order to help calm them down. There is no explanation for who conjured up that sort of treatment. There definitely needs to be some level of reassessment on that, because it doesn't make things better. It might in the long run, but it most certainly does NOT please the soul during the short run. Your hands start shaking, and you fear the second that liquid makes contact with the eyeball, and you just want so desperately for it all to be over. So, by the time you get the intestinal fortitude to suck it up and deal, you have now covered your entire face in the liquid ointment, because you have been twitching and moving too much to control where the little droplets are going. I who wore glasses and contacts for nearly 20 years, had corrective eye surgery, and loved every second of it. I have never been squeamish or had an issue playing with my eyeballs until then. While having surgery, I got to smell my eyeballs burning, but was too doped up on valium to really care. Plus, as everything came into focus it was a transformational moment. I think I managed to happily yell, "I can see!" And yet, that was nothing.

Nevertheless, the experience is one of those things that introduces humility into your life. You begin to realize that things really can take a person down to their knees, and after watching a multitude of people go through the same series of events, I can honestly tell you it is comical. You also realize that your body has a way of doing whatever it wants, without your control.

The level of snot that comes out of your orifices is simply shocking. Your eyes don't want to open despite your best efforts to, and meanwhile you have geniuses that shout "open your eyes" at you, as if that's even a remote possibility at that second. Eventually they just give up and say, "follow the sound of my voice", as they lead you from obstacle to obstacle. If they are tremendously unlucky, they will get distracted and a snot-drooling zombie that they are supposed to leading the correct way will run face first into them. I have seen that happen. And the volunteer that agreed to help the latest batch of zombies realizes that they have now been blessed with the biological secretions of another, all down the back or side of their shirt. Then they usually make the greatest faces of all time. Disgust comes in many forms! Even though it is their fault, they usually proceed to get mad at the person who has just face bumped their guide, in an effort to follow their voice, and instructions, only to stop abruptly and wonder why the heck they are running into things. Those with courage will try and justify their blind actions. Those without will just take the verbal ass-whopping and try and blend into the fold for the remainder of the time allotted for the course and recovery.

When you see a certified bad ass bow down to his knees and start pleading to make it stop, you start panicking inside. There's a certain degree of intestinal fortitude within everyone, and I have seen some of the biggest, most assertive persons get taken out. Meanwhile, you have teeny tots who have not a lick of muscle on them, and are generally perceived as weak, blow through the course like nothing happened. Are they in pain, yes. Are they aware that they are going to live through it, yes. And they just do what needs to be done and worry about the pain later. Yet again, I say life has a funny way of showing us who has invisible qualities and who doesn't. Pepper spray has no mercy. It will be a similar feeling for everyone, but the reactions are always drastically different. There is no preparing yourself for how you may handle it, but it is always surprising to see which personalities make it their bitch, and who are made the bitch.

Chapter 26

It is Not What Love Is, But What Love Can Be

Just last week I would have told anyone that love is more of a commercial enterprise in this day and age than anything else. The idea that two people can love each other the "right" way, truly devoted to one another, was not something I could fathom. Until I had an epiphany. Twenty years ago, my heart broke for the first time (at least for my conscious self). The day I left Indonesia I had to say goodbye to someone who showed me infinite kindness, true devotion, and loved me as if I were her own kid. Her name is Lena. This woman welcomed me into her heart and her life gradually over time, after being hired on to care for me. She and I had a special connection, a rare one. We taught each other our respective languages and tested the boundaries of what a family truly is. She kept me in line, demonstrated sympathy and empathy when necessary, but she also truly understood me. I felt myself around her. I could be honest and be heard, and inspired by what I could do for myself, with a push in the right direction. Which, for all intents and purposes, is what love can be.

Before I get ahead of myself, let's back up a bit. It is my belief that love has never been a positive influence in the lives of the majority of people I have encountered. I have seen abusive relationships left and right, people seeking to control and harm in order to defend what is perceived to be their territory. I have also seen people desire to be with someone, and called it love. Yet they may have mistaken it for loneliness. I have also met others who have no idea who they are, because they are so consumed by what another person means to them, in the name of love. For these reasons, and many more, I believed love to be a concept, an ideal, but certainly not a reality for many. Although following my revolutionary thoughts as of late, I am beginning to rethink this well-conceived notion of mine.

For reasons unknown to me, I have been loved over the years in a multitude of fashions. I have been unprepared for it; I have been unaware of it until it snuck up on me and slapped me in the face. I have also been completely consumed by it, and I have been wrong to identify my feelings as love. Over the years I had become a cynic. I did not believe in a story-book romance, or someone would sweep me off my feet. But I did believe in being the best human being I could. Therefore, I was satisfied with that for a long time. Although I was never really prepared for it, I like to think love eventually found me a time or two. But more so in ways I least expected. Love truly challenged my notions about relationships, and not just the physically intimate type. I have realized that in demonstrating kindness and assisting others, bonds form. People open up and trust is unearthed and eventually groomed. Before long, you stop wondering about whether or not someone will like you, because by the time you realize it, you've already shown them your weakest or most horrid moments. At this moment, most people run away. I know I have. For me, showing anyone anything other than perfection was never an option.

I recently saw this video on Facebook of all places, that asked women what type of female they were. Were they the ones who wore a mask and demonstrated perfection, were they the type to please others rather than standing up for their own thoughts and expectations, or were they the ones who were shy and kept to themselves? I identified most with the person who showed perfection, so I believed that to be me. As the video went on, it quickly turned on me. It explained that despite preconceived notions, all women demonstrate every aspect of each, depending upon moods. And it hit me, that makes sense! Who would have thought Facebook videos would provide enlightening content? As soon as I got over that shock, I knew exactly what that meant for me, and my ideals about love. There are moments we all hope to put our best foot forward, there are alternative moments when we give in. And there are also moments when we don't need or even want to be around others for fear that we may not live up to their expectations. That we might disappoint somehow and experience betrayal. For me, this clarifies the notions I have had about love. Love is the ability to accept those who are in their perfect moments, their weakest or most vulnerable and simultaneously nasty selves, and also give them space to be themselves. Love is a connection that does not limit another person, yet it empowers them to grow, to exceed all expectations and limits, to push another out of their comfort zone, and to make change. Whether it turn out positive, or negative. But to try and assist them in becoming a better human being, to strengthen perceived weaknesses and to encourage strengths.

Ironically, Lena showed me just that. She saw me when I was up to no good, and trust that I was up to no good. She witnessed me when I was happy and freespirited, and she also would come check on me when I was feeling down and didn't want anyone around. She demonstrated care and concern through her actions time and time again, that I was not just the daughter of a client. That I was someone who mattered to her, both for her wellbeing and mine. Lena pushed me repeatedly out of my comfort zone, and I did the same to her. I always asked her to let me help her do housework and let me eat dinner with her, which to her was socially unacceptable. She kept me in check when I would get out of control and start pressing buttons and doing things I knew would gain negative attention. Lena kept me out of harm's way - from myself and others. She would rub my back until I was asleep at night, and she would come save me from things I was not comfortable around, like spiders. I would taunt her with geckos and snails, while she would scare me with rats and assorted critters that she would save us from (with a broom, no less). Lena would sneak me candy every now and again, so I could enjoy some of the finer things in life during my childhood, because to her, kids deserved treats. She would parent me, and I accepted. That was our bond for our three years together. Of course, the day she was forced to say goodbye was just as painful as it was for me. And while I don't know if it resonated with her as much it has with me, I find comfort in knowing that it was never about anything less than being human.

Lena was from a very different religious and cultural background, yet none of that mattered. She didn't understand the western way of doing things, and idolized America, and I would tell her stories about the different states, and where to go. Everything I remember, not because of what she was on the outside, or because of identifiable connotations, was because of who she was towards me. It occurred to me shortly after I left Indonesia that I didn't even know her last name. Yet, her heart was just as big as mine, and to me that will always be what love is.

Fast forward a few years from my childhood in Indonesia, and you will find another occasion worth reflecting upon. I met a friend, who I will call Mike for the purposes of this book. Mike worked at a local place that I frequented a lot throughout high school, and even some afterwards. He and I grew a friendship through similar interests, and we eventually became more than friends. Not necessarily committed to each other, in the traditional sense, but for argument's sake we will call it friends with benefits. He was present in a time of my life when I needed someone. Mike had a way of enjoying life and trying to reduce the chaos and drama. So, I quickly felt at ease whenever I could just take a step out of a situation and exist in that moment. I found refuge around him quite a lot. He proved on more than one occasion to be a very amazing friend, helping me when I was in dire straits. Though we didn't always communicate regularly, we still keep in touch. After a period of time, we reconnected and remained in touch more consistently in the past, and Mike proved himself to be somewhat of a refuge for me, once again.

There are not many people in my life that I keep in touch with on a regular basis. That sounds terrible, but I usually find three or four close friends and I stick with them. However, when someone moves on or out of the area, regular communication tends to slip to the wayside. I think most would agree with me when I say that is relatively reasonable. But for me personally, there are even less people who know me from my young days, from over two decades ago, and Mike is one. He saw things that even he could not explain. Mike saw me at my worst, my best, and then some. He heard what people said about me behind my back yet demonstrated the ability to give me a chance to prove my worth, as a human. When someone lets rumors and complex dynamics go to the wayside and gives another a chance, well, let's just say that's a rare breed!

Although we haven't seen each other in years, every time we pick up the phone, it is as if time has not passed. Mike is just as much a friend, an older brother-figure, and confidant as he has always been. While we may have had moments within our friendship that were more intimate than others, both physically and not so, there is never a moment where our friendship wasn't worth fighting for. In this day and age, I find that people are less likely to be able to separate friendship from relationship. For us, the physical relationship was never the sole purpose of our continued connection. We were friends first, only intimate a few times, and were able to keep on going without skipping a beat. This might seem weird to some, but for us it works. For us, we have value in each other, and when you can say you've known someone for almost 20 years, and you're just over 30 that means something! For me, this relationship we have concocted for ourselves is a demonstration of love because nothing else has stood in the way. Time, distance, emotions, trials and tribulations, and conflict have all been a part of our dynamic. With that much time spent getting to know a person, how can anyone resist keeping them in their lives? There's always something that you will disagree upon, and there's always some test during the course of time that will challenge your devotion and will to another, yet nothing has torn us apart that we cannot mend. We have proven as much, time and time again.

The next encounter I will divulge will probably be the last. (Since I've already discussed my husband, there's little to no point of beating a dead horse.) These next two people will be Kevin and Todd, for the purposes of my story. Both are older men that I know. During the time I hung out regularly with both of these people as friends, there was a lot going on in all our lives. There is some overlap here, with regards to time, so bear with me. I do not think they knew each other, however we hung out in the same places. Though my relationship with Kevin was very different than my friendship with Todd, I discuss them together because there was a bond that existed with each man that resonates a strong similarity. The connection I mean is one that is of an undying devotion. There are moments of true vulnerability shared, in words, between myself and Kevin, and also with myself and Todd. Though we might not have been in the same mindset as one another at the time, they also shared the same struggles I was going through. The also confessed similar secrets during our friendship that sort of bonded us in a way unlike any other. To each other, we became the reason for getting up in the morning.

It is hard to explain to anyone who has never suffered from depression, what depression is like. Saying the words doesn't exactly do the feeling justice. Being so down that you have considered hurting yourself, well that's even lower. To find another person who has experienced that within one lifetime is not necessarily difficult. However, to find an individual willing to talk about your specific circumstances in grave detail, well, there's just nothing else like it. You earn yourself an understanding of that person, deep within them, that no one else deserves to know, unless it is by their tongue. That information stays between the two of you, and from then on, you possess an insight to them that others might not. With both Kevin and Todd, this relationship existed for me. It was mutual, with both men. They let me in, just as much as I let them in. And for all intents and purposes, we knew that letting each other down wasn't an option. So even in our darkest of moments, when there was no hope left, there was that light at the end of the tunnel to get us through it all. That bonds people together similar to the way soldiers engaged in battle will be eternally bonded.

This type of love is not something you find walking down the street. The ability to connect down to the core like that is not done by denying yourself the ability to understand what you want or need. So, many people are not incapable of achieving that connection. Certain people just tend to see things differently and shrinks frequently call that denial. To be honest with yourself is hard. This is an understatement. To be honest at a core level with not one, but two individuals, well, that's just crazy. Never before had I experienced that. Even to this day both men mean the world to me. They are crazy characters, who will literally never tell a soul what we went through, and exactly what we know. The devotion towards each other is a connection I believe is only possible when love exists. Otherwise, why keep the secret?

Love has always managed to amaze me when I least expected it. In these circumstances, I had all but given up hope. To say I was in a dark spot in my life would be an understatement. Yet, the powers to be chose to give me a reason to survive. They handed me a connection that I will forever value. Two, even! As I have said, I am very difficult to kill, because somehow the universe has kept me alive through insurmountable odds, and most of the time coincidences like this have occurred. What I needed was provided for me not only when I least expected it, but through forms completely unbeknownst to me. I never once looked at either of these individuals and thought, "I'm going to have a wicked close moment with him". Yet, here I am today, writing about it. I guess if nothing else, I lived to tell the tale!

I guess what I'm trying to say is, you never know what is around the corner, or how to define a term, until you experience it. And recognize the qualities of said experience on your own. For me, I spent much of my life not experiencing a love that I needed. For many years I felt as though I would never get married, have kids, bond with another human being. Ironically, I thought I would never make it that far. Yet years later, here I am. I survived. I experienced love that not only made me question what traditional family roles can be, but also the role of a friend over the course of time, and friends of opposite genders. There isn't a single person who can tell me what love is. Just as I can't necessarily dictate to you what you believe love to be. But as I mentioned earlier, it is an undeniable force that breaks you out of what you know and are comfortable with and encourages you to improve upon yourself. Sure, there are folks that claim to love another individual, yet smother their existence by tracking their every second, interaction, movement and possibly even resorting to physical violence. You can't convince me that that is love. True love is meant to be pure in nature. It is not meant to harm. That would be better defined as control, jealousy, and rage. Maybe even fear.

Love is best represented in my opinion, in the five-letter word, smile. Though there are various forms of a smile that have negative connotations, like smirk or sneer, I am talking about a genuine smile. Something that is truly only accomplished by happiness. When your face lights up at the sight of someone you haven't seen all day. Or a joke that makes you laugh until your stomach hurts. Smiling is a simple concept, but it demands a presence of positivity and hope that many other impressions do not give. You cannot derive either from a stare, glance or movement. But you can immediately discern what someone is feeling when you see their teeth through an upward grin. You know that something good is going to happen. Awareness of what a simple act can demonstrate is just the beginning of what a smile can accomplish when it comes to love, and vice versa. A smile can mean reassurance, confidence, pleasure, and devotion. I can even be in love and flash a smile to make that person's day improve two-fold. Or I can smile and accomplish the same to a perfect stranger. In either circumstance, it is impossible to wind up negatively affected by someone's genuine smile. Smiling is the most intense demonstration of love, and what better way is there to reveal your feelings for someone if not by encouraging and fostering true love?

— Conclusion —

In closing, it is apparent that the idea of what is normal is flexible, considerably flexible. I do not claim to be the all-knowing, by any means. Yet I find inspiration in other people's stories and experiences and understand that normal is based upon your personal experiences just as much as anyone else's. Those who grow up with a reality like mine do not fit the typical mold and frequently struggle to submerge themselves into the social world. They frequently possess emotions they cannot control, and do not know how to express within the confines of appropriate behavior. Nevertheless, some of us pull through and can blend to the best of our ability, and others end up incarcerated or worse.

Though I have been blessed with the opportunity to explore other countries and cultures I still yearn for the opportunity to find that calling that pulls me in and never lets go. Maybe I will find that in parenthood. Who knows really? Honestly, finding a higher purpose is not only based on the individual, and how they can hold faith and value in something that is possibly not quite as significant to another. All in all, life is what we make of it. You can choose to learn something from every occurrence or piece of advice, or you can choose to ignore it all and carry on.

Denial exists in this world to challenge us all. Recognizing that some are incapable of facing reality is hard to deal with, and at times not worth your time. Nevertheless, to help another person and aid them in times of need and personal discovery seems to be what I've resorted to for now. I am fully aware of my surroundings, my allies and demons, and my potential shortcomings. I choose to rise above the petty sentiments and face greater challenges with my eyes and heart wide open.

One thing I know for certain is, we are all human. Human nature possesses failure. It possesses breakdowns and strife. Life has its way with us and then spits us out. That is all normal. Being human also includes being sexual, having joyous moments of accomplishment, and moments of sorrow. Having a moratorium phase to explore oneself and alcohol, and maybe even drugs too. No one should feel less of a person for experiencing all that life has to offer. It is true that everything in moderation is probably best, but for those who are unable to control the urges they usually possess their own struggle. I feel it is best not to judge, and let life takes its course. I harbor no ill will to any individuals who have done me wrong, and I am a better person for it. I figure life will have a way of handling them in due time, and I do not need to be taken down to their level for harboring a grudge. Being able to separate myself from what is truly not my fault enables me to remain healthy. Respecting myself and what I possess inside and continuing to stand true to my morals is how I enable myself to continue with my head held high.

I guess the purpose of this autobiography is to be honest, maybe even brutally honest. In a way, I think we all need reassurance that we are not pieces of shit. That we are able to find refuge in the experiences and similarities of other people around us. We are after all, social beings, right? Solace can be found through a variety of avenues, be it journaling, meditation, counseling or therapy, friends, and even family. Having someone there to listen can at times be the greatest achievement of all. It is a motivating factor for us to push through the less than brilliant moments of our lives, and if I reach one person with this book I feel as though maybe, just maybe, I have contributed positively to the world. To the point where something beneficial can be discerned. If I have been able to cause a moment of laughter and wonder, then I have become successful. Although I have written many papers, writing down my thoughts and feelings has not necessarily been easy, yet it is a form of healing. Urging others to find ways to heal is also another goal, for this is something that only the strongest people are willing to achieve. Whether or not we admit it to ourselves, everyone has a potential component that makes them useful in this world. Whether anyone has told you, YOU matter. If you have not lived through nearly the same kind of traumas or positive experiences, you are still just as important as the next person. You have something to offer the world. You just need to look within and find what matters to you most. After spending years "behind" everyone else, in a way, it was different trying to discover my own desires and failures, but in due time everyone is perfectly normal. They are fantastic, and that should never be diminished or forgotten.